TEACH YOURSELF BOOKS

PHOTOSHOP

Trademarks

Many of the designations used by manufacturers and sellers to distinguish their products are claimed as trademarks. Where those designations appear in this book, and Hodder and Stoughton was aware of the trademark claim, the designations have been printed in initial caps or all caps.

Long-renowned as the authoritative source for self-guided learning – with more than 30 million copies sold worldwide – the *Teach Yourself* series includes over 200 titles in the fields of languages, crafts, hobbies, sports, and other leisure activities.

Catalogue entry for this title is available from the British Library.

Library of Congress Catalog Card Number on file

First published in UK 1997 by Hodder Headline Plc, 338 Euston Road, London NW1 3BH

First published in US 1997 by NTC Publishing Group
An imprint of NTC/Contemporary Publishing Company
4255 West Touhy Avenue, Lincolnwood (Chicago), Illinois 60646 – 1975 U.S.A.

The 'Teach Yourself' name and logo are registered trade marks of Hodder & Stoughton Ltd in the UK.

Printed in Great Britain by Cox & Wyman Ltd, Reading, Berkshire.

Impression number	10 9 8 7 6 5 4 3 2
Year	2000 1999 1998 1997

CONTENTS

1

INTRODUCTION

This book has a simple purpose: to introduce complete beginners to digital image processing using Adobe Photoshop 4.0 and teach the necessary skills they will need to scan, retouch, enhance and compose still images.

In aiming to give readers a good grounding in the use of the program, I have concentrated on those controls, techniques and processes essential to the creation of sound, well-balanced imagery, whatever the subject matter or final use.

Multimedia in all its manifestations has meant that the computer has become a medium in its own right rather than just a tool. Digital images are now as likely to be integrated into web pages and multimedia projects as into DTP documents and I have kept this in mind throughout the book.

Whilst the version discussed is Photoshop 4.0, most of the procedures I cover can be achieved within version 3.0, as I have only included those new features of version 4.0 which are likely to be suitable for first-time users.

Whether you are new to visual communications or already work in the graphic arts field, I hope you will find the book a useful guide to a remarkable image-processing tool.

—— Overview of Photoshop ——

What is Photoshop?

Photoshop is an digital image-processing program, providing the user with a single environment in which scanning, retouching and image enhancement can be accomplished.

It includes:
resizing and mode controls
selection and masking facilities
painting and editing tools
pasting and layer controls
tonal and colour correction controls
special effect filters
powerful colour conversion capabilities.

Bitmapped images

Photoshop processes bitmapped images, which are created using scanning or digital photographic methods. A bitmapped image can be described as a mosaic of picture elements, each element representing a single tone or colour.

Mode and resolution

Whether elements within an image are just black or white, or use a range of tones or colours is determined by its mode. The density of picture elements (the number of elements or pixels per inch) is determined by its resolution.

The attributes of mode, resolution and overall dimensions are set at the scanning or photographic stage but are alterable at any time.

Paint effects

You can colour images using the painting tools in combination with the selection tools. These tools also enable you to originate and modify masks.

Retouching attributes

You can retouch images using the editing tools in combination with selection and painting tools. These tools enable you to remove unwanted details within images or improve on existing details.

Layers

You can cut and paste images within and between documents and create multi-layered documents for complex montaging work. When pasting, you can rotate, flip, scale and distort images using the transformation commands.

Tonal, colour and sharpness attributes

You can improve the tonal values, colour balance, saturation, brightness and sharpness of an image using the Adjust controls and sharpening filters.

Text, borders and panels

You can add type to an image using the type tool and make simple graphic elements, such as borders and vignetted panels, using selection tools in combination with the border, stroke and feather commands.

Outputting to print

You can output documents to desktop printers for proofing or imageset documents to bromide or colour separations.

You can convert colour images to the CMYK printing mode and save images in appropriate file formats for importing to DTP documents.

Saving for multimedia

You can save images in appropriate file formats for use in web pages, interactive presentations and multimedia projects.

Conventions used in this book

Keystrokes in the main text are shown as icons [⌘]

When icons are separated by a + sign, as in [⌘][Alt]+[F], the modifier key(s) before the + sign should be held down, whilst the key after the + sign is pressed.

Some keyboards include an [Option] instead of the [Alt] key.

Photoshop images are reproduced in varying resolutions throughout the book to communicate different points.

Other margin icons in this book are used in the following contexts.

●   Single-step instructions and key points.

①   Step-by-step instructions.

!   Warnings and critical information.

▲   Helpful hints.

✚   Additional non-essential information.

2

THE PHOTOSHOP INTERFACE

This chapter covers:

- the document window
- the Tool, Brushes and Options palettes
- the scroll bars, menu and dialog boxes

Photoshop interface

This chapter is intended as a general reference to several features of the Photoshop interface, including the Photoshop document window and the Tool, Brushes and Options palettes.

For those new to the Macintosh, it includes a sub-section on the standard Macintosh controls used within the program.

You may wish just to peruse this chapter and move on, referring back to it as and when necessary.

The document window

The document window displays an open Photoshop image.

Features include:

① title bar
② close box
③ zoom box
④ size box
⑤ image area
⑥ scroll bars
⑦ rulers
⑧ ruler origin
⑨ file sizes
⑩ mode
⑪ scale/scale field
⑫ page preview box.

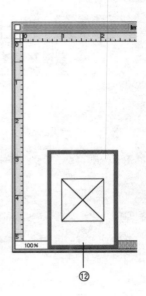

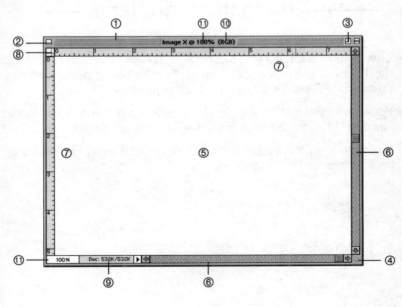

The tool palette

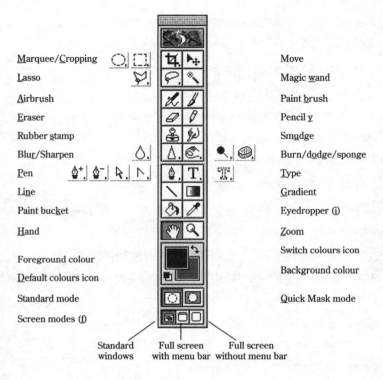

Marquee/Cropping	Move
Lasso	Magic wand
Airbrush	Paint brush
Eraser	Pencil y
Rubber stamp	Smudge
Blur/Sharpen	Burn/dodge/sponge
Pen	Type
Line	Gradient
Paint bucket	Eyedropper (i)
Hand	Zoom
	Switch colours icon
Foreground colour	
Default colours icon	Background colour
Standard mode	Quick Mask mode
Screen modes (f)	

Standard windows   Full screen with menu bar   Full screen without menu bar

Underlined letters are tool short-cuts

Selecting a tool

● Click once to select a tool. The pointer changes to the tool cursor. Click or click-drag on the image as appropriate.

▲ Press the Caps Lock key to turn icons into a cross hair pointer for precision working.

Select tools sharing the same location within the palette by either holding down the Alt key and clicking or click-dragging to the tool in the 'pop-up' menu.

Press the Command key to access the Move tool temporarily. Press the underlined letters above for shortcuts to each tool.

Tools overview

Marquee: for selecting rectangular and elliptical areas

Cropping: for cropping an image

Move: for moving selections and layers

Lasso: for selecting free form areas

Magic Wand: for selecting areas of similar colour

Airbrush: for spraying with soft edges

Paint brush: for painting with soft edges

Eraser: for exposing the background colour

Pencil(y): for drawing and retouching with hard edges

Rubber stamp: for cloning parts of an image

Focussing tools (r): for blurring and sharpening areas

Toning tools: for altering the brightness and saturation of areas

Smudge: for smudging areas

Pen: for drawing paths

Type: for entering type

Line: for drawing straight lines

Gradient: for graduating colours

Paint bucket: for filling areas of a pre-defined colour range

Eyedropper (i): for selecting current colours

Hand: for scrolling the image within the document window

Zoom: for altering the viewing scale

▲   Press the underlined letters for short-cuts to each tool.

！   The Move and Cropping tools differ in functionality between Photoshop 3.0 and Photoshop 4.0. The Pen tool is accessed through the Paths palette in Photoshop 3.0.

Fine-tuning tools

Tool performance is controlled by settings in the Options and Brushes palettes. Both palette contents vary from tool to tool.

The palettes can be collapsed to take up less screen space by clicking on their Zoom boxes.

The Brushes palette

Brush settings alter the size and shape – the 'tip'– of a tool.

Altering a tip

① Choose Show Brushes in the Window menu.

② Click on a standard hard (or soft-edged) 'tip' option.

③ Click-drag the tool over the image.

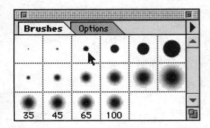

The Options palette

Settings in the Options palette alter the effect of a tool – the degree a tool alters an image or, in the case of selection tools, the size and character of a selection. Some tools have settings for attributes unique to the tool. These settings are covered elsewhere.

Altering the strength of a tool

① Select a tool.

② Choose Show Options in the Window menu.

③ Move the slider on the Options palette (if any).

④ Click-drag the tool over the image.

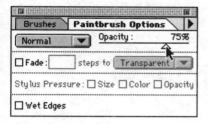

▲ Press 1 – 0 on keyboard to set the opacity, pressure etc for any tool.

Some tools can be used in different modes. Like opacity, tool pressure and exposure, modes also control how colours replace underlying pixels in an image; e.g. Darken mode restricts changes to darker values, ignoring colours lighter than the underlying image. Modes can be used in combination with opacity etc. to achieve unusual overlay effects. See *Blending Modes* (page 125).

Altering the mode of a tool

① Choose Show Options in the Window menu.

② Choose an option in the Mode pop-up menu.

③ Click-drag the tool over the image.

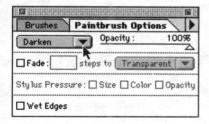

Macintosh basics

Scroll bars

Every window within Photoshop has two scroll bars, one for vertical scrolling and one for horizontal scrolling. A grey scroll bar indicates more content beyond a window's borders; a clear bar indicates all content is visible.

Using the scroll bars

● Click the up, down, left or right scroll arrow.

Or:

● Click the vertical or horizontal scroll bar on either side of the scroll box, when it's grey.

Or:

● Drag the vertical or horizontal scroll box along its scroll bar.

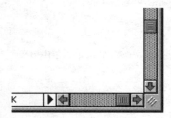

Menus

Menus within Photoshop come in two types: pull-down menus and pop-up menus. The menus in the Photoshop menu bar are pull-down menus. Pop-up menus often appear in palettes and dialog boxes.

Selecting options from pull-down menus

● Point to the menu name, press to 'pull down' the menu, drag to the item you wish to choose so that it's highlighted and then release the mouse button.

Dialog boxes

In general, dialog boxes provide a means of specifying and applying image attributes. You can enter specifications into these boxes in a number of ways.

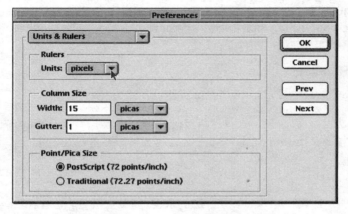

Dialog box with pop-up menus, fields and radio buttons.

Entering new values in fields

①   Double-click existing values (if not already highlighted).

②   Type in new values.

Moving from field to field

●   Press [Tab]

Selecting options from pop-up menus

●   Point to the visible menu item, press to 'pop up' the menu, drag to the item you wish to choose so that it's highlighted and then release the mouse button.

Checking boxes

●   Click the box. An X indicates that it's selected.

Clicking radio buttons

●   Click the button. A emboldened button indicates that it's selected.

Resetting specifications in dialog boxes

●   Hold down [Alt] to replace Cancel by Reset. Click Reset.

Applying specifications and closing box

●   Click OK or press [Return] or [Enter ↵]

Undoing work

You can correct mistakes in a number of ways in Photoshop.

Undoing a minor action

●   Choose Undo... in the Edit menu.

❗   Photoshop can only undo the very last action by this means.

Undoing a series of actions

You can undo a series of actions by reverting to the saved file on disk. If you use this method, it's important to save in a tactical way, anticipating the use of this command.

①   Choose Revert in the File menu. An alert box saying 'Revert to a previously saved version of "..." ?' will be displayed.

②   Click Revert to revert to saved. Click Cancel if you do not wish to revert.

▲   You can use the Rubber Stamp tool to paint parts of an image back to how it looked when the file was last saved or back to a Snapshot. You can also use the Eraser tool to 'paint back' parts of an image. See *Undoing retouching work* (page 91).

3

OPENING AND
SAVING IMAGES

This chapter covers:

- the Open directory dialog box
- the Save As directory dialog box
- the Save a Copy directory dialog box
- the New Document dialog box

Loading Photoshop

- Double-click on the Photoshop™ program icon within the Photoshop folder on your hard disk.

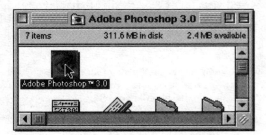

‼ There is no need to double-click the icon if it's greyed as this indicates that Photoshop is already loaded on the RAM.

See *Allocating memory* if Photoshop informs you of a lack of memory.

Opening an existing image

Photoshop can open digitally photographed and scanned images in many file formats, including PICT, TIFF, EPS, Photo CD and JPEG.

Either:

① Choose Open… in the Photoshop's File menu. The Open directory dialog box will be displayed.

‼ If the Photoshop menu is not showing, choose Photoshop in the Applications menu at the far right of the menu bar. If it not listed, load Photoshop – see *Loading Photoshop*. The menu bar in Photoshop 3.0 differs in detail to the bar in Photoshop 4.0.

② Use the directory dialog box controls to locate your image.

③ If an image is not listed, choose All Files the format pop-up menu or check Show all files.

④ Click Open. The document window will be displayed.

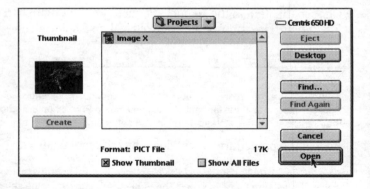

Or:

● Double-click on its document icon in its Finder window, if it's a Photoshop document. The document window will be displayed.

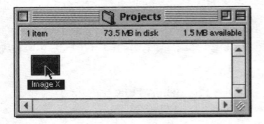

❢ Only open images within a Finder window if they have been previously saved within Photoshop.

✚ If Photoshop has not already been loaded on the RAM it will now be loaded. Its title and menu bar will be displayed in a few moments.

See *Allocating memory* if Photoshop informs you of a lack of memory.

Acquiring images

Kodak Photo CD and digital camera images can be directly accessed and opened via Plug-in or TWAIN modules.

① Choose the item in the Import sub-menu in the Photoshop's File menu. The appropriate controls will be displayed.

❢ If the Photoshop menu is not showing, choose Photoshop in the Applications menu at the far right of the menu bar. In Photoshop 3.0, choose the Acquire sub-menu instead of the Import sub-menu.

② Follow the procedure as laid down by the manufacturer.

❢ Plug-ins and TWAIN drivers need to be placed in the Import/Export folder within Photoshop's Plug-ins folder. The Plug-ins folder needs to be selected within the Plug-ins and Scratch Disks Preferences dialog box for the appropriate command to be listed in the Import or Acquire sub-menu.

Resaving an image

●   Chose Save... in the File menu.

▲   Resave every five minutes or so whilst you are working on an image, always using the Save command. The Save As directory dialog box will not be displayed.

Creating a copy of an image

Use this process to create and move to a copy of a document.

①   Chose Save As... in the File menu. The Save As directory dialog box will be displayed.

②   Enter a document name, overwriting its existing name.

③   Choose an option in the Format pop-up menu.

④   Select a drive and folder in which to save the file.

⑤   Click Save to save the document. Click Cancel if you wish to abort the routine.

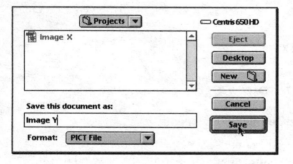

!   If you wish the new document to contain all your latest work, choose Save... in the File menu first and then choose Save As...

▲   Although you can use up to 31 characters in a file name, it's best to restrict yourself to around 20 so that names appear in full within directory dialog boxes.

Saving a copy of an image

Use this process to save a flattened version of a layered document. See *Montaging images*.

①   Choose Save a Copy… in the File menu. The Save a Copy directory dialog box will be displayed.

②   Enter a new document name, overwriting the existing name.

③   Choose an option other than Photoshop 3.0 in the Format pop-up menu. Flatten image will automatically be checked.

④   Select a drive and folder in which to save the file.

⑤   Click Save to save the flattened document. Click Cancel if you wish to abort the routine.

Closing an image

①   Click the Close box at the top left of the document window.

②   An alert box saying 'Save the new document "…"?' or 'Save changes to document "…"?' will be displayed if recent work has not been saved.

③   Click OK.

Quitting Photoshop

①   Choose Quit in the File menu.

②   An alert box saying 'Save the new document "…"?' or 'Save changes to document "…"?' will be displayed if your document is still open and recent work has not been saved.

③   Click OK.

Creating a blank document

You can create a blank document in which to paste images from other documents. If an image is already on the Clipboard, the settings in the New dialog box will automatically match its dimensions, resolution and mode.

① Choose New in Photoshop's File menu. The New dialog box will be displayed.

! If the Photoshop menu is not showing, choose Photoshop in the Applications menu at the far right of the menu bar.

② Enter a name in the Name field (this is optional).

③ Choose an option in the Units pop-up menus.

④ Enter values into the Width and Height fields.

⑤ Choose an option in the Mode pop-up menu.

⑥ Click an option under Contents. If you select Transparent, the document will consist of a single layer. See Chapter 12, *Montaging images*.

⑦ Click OK. The document window will be displayed.

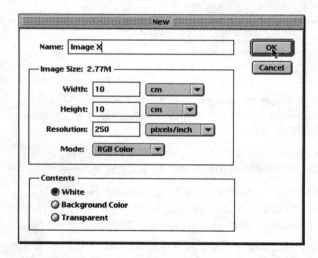

▲ When you are entering values into fields in dialog boxes, it's best to double-click the existing values to highlight them, and then to enter the new value to overwrite them.

Saving a new document

Before you do any work in your new document, give it a name (if it has not already been named) and save it to disk.

①   Chose Save... in the File menu. The Save As directory dialog box will be displayed.

②   Enter a document name, overwriting the name Untitled-1, unless it is already named.

③   Select a drive and folder in which to save the file.

④   Click Save to save the document. Click Cancel if you wish to abort the routine.

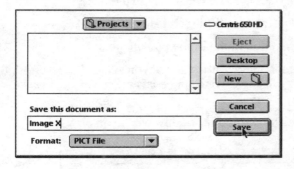

Summary:

●   **Always open an image using Photoshop's Open command unless the image is already a Photoshop document.**

●   **Give documents descriptive names, preferably no longer than 20 characters, including spaces.**

●   **Create blank documents by choosing New in Photoshop's File menu. Its attributes will automatically match any image on the Clipboard.**

●   **Before making a copy of a document, save normally, if you wish the original document to include your most recent work.**

4

THE SCANNING PROCESS

This chapter covers:

- scanning controls
- the Save As directory dialog box
- the Image Size dialog box

—— Scanning considerations ——

Scanning is a method of capturing images in digitised form. Once scanned, images can be placed in DTP documents, interactive presentations or multimedia projects.

You can scan any images provided they are flat and not too big. Usually images are in the form of colour transparencies, photographic prints, printed material or flat artwork.

Types of scanner

Transparencies are scanned using transmissive scanners, whereas prints and flat artwork are scanned using reflective scanners.

In transmissive scanners, light passes through the transparent image, whereas in reflective scanners light is reflected off the surface of the image.

In both types, the varying intensities of light are usually converted into electrical charges by Charged-Coupled Device technology (CCD for short). These charges are then converted to digital data.

When using a scanner, ensure its optical resolution is adequate for the work you wish to do (See *Scanning accurately*). Resolution is described as either optical or optical supplemented by interpolated; interpolation is used to resample optically-recorded data during the scanning process.

Some scanners are described as having two optical resolutions, such as 300×400 ppi (dpi). The lower figure represents the number of CCD elements across the scanner bed, the higher figure represents the number of recorded steps the CCD takes to pass down the length of the bed. In such cases, the lower figure, in this case 300, is often interpolated to match the higher figure, in this case 400. This gives a better result than an optical resolution of 300 in both directions.

Make sure you use a scanner which supports 24-bit or above. This will enable you to scan in full colour (recording over 16 million colours) as well as in grayscale and line.

!   If you scan an image at 48-bit, you will need to reduce its depth to 24 within Photoshop 4.0 before you can use most of the program's commands. Do this by choosing 8 bits/Channel in the Mode sub-menu in the Image menu.

✦   Some desktop scanners are hybrid, combining both reflective and transmissive methods.

Scanning controls and terminology

Scanning controls and terminology can vary considerably from scanner to scanner. You will find some controls are fairly intuitive; others not very logically laid out. It may take you time to familiarise yourself with the main controls on your scanner but it's time well spent if you wish to work efficiently.

Terminology can present a problem as manufacturers use different words to describe the same things, especially the level of colour in images. This attribute can be variously described as:

1-bit; line; bitmap: black and white

8-bit; grayscale: black and white photo

24-bit; colour: millions of colours

32-bit and 48-bit; colour: billions of colours

1-bit refers to images which contain only black and white areas.

8-bit refers to images which contain 256 shades of grey, including black and white.

24-bit refers to images which contain over 16.7 million colours.

Both 32-bit and 48-bit refer to images which contain billions of colours.

The terms line, black and white photo and colour are also used to describe the quality of originals.

Scanning from within Photoshop

Most scanners come with versions of their software drivers in the form of Photoshop-compatible plug-ins. Some come with generic TWAIN drivers. Either system allows you to load and access scanning controls from within Photoshop itself. This is the best way to scan: it's seamless, with scanned images automatically converted into Photoshop documents.

You can, if you wish, scan an image independently of Photoshop by loading the scanning program directly. If you do this the final scanned image will need to be saved in TIFF format, uncompressed and then closed. You can then re-open the image within Photoshop for further processing. See *Opening an existing image.*

There is no qualitative difference between the two approaches; the former approach is just quicker and more convenient.

!   Plug-ins and TWAIN drivers need to be placed in the Import/Export folder within Photoshop's Plug-ins folder. The Plug-ins folder needs to be selected within the Plug-ins and Scratch Disks Preferences dialog box for the appropriate command to be listed in the Import or Acquire sub-menu.

Scanning attributes

The scanning process involves setting certain image attributes, whatever the make of your scanner. These attributes define the dimensions, level of colour (bit-depth) and density of data in the final image.

These can be listed as:

● Crop (area of the original to be scanned)

● Dimensions (final dimensions of scanned image)

● Bit-depth (whether line, grayscale or colour information is to be recorded)

● Resolution (density of data recorded in scanned image).

—— The scanning process ——

The features referred to in the following process may differ from your scanning controls. Refer to the user manual which came with your scanner for operational instructions specific to your machine.

Ensure that your scanning program is set to its default calibration unless it has been professionally re-calibrated.

Brightness, gamma and colour settings should be neutral and any sharpening control should be disabled.

Making a scan

Inserting an original

① Place a transparency/negative or print/artwork in the appropriate position in your scanner.

In the case of a transparency/negative, place the item in the carrier provided. In the case of a print/artwork, position the item on the scanner glass.

Loading the scanning program

② Choose your scanner in the Import sub-menu in the File menu. The menu will normally list the scanner name preceded by the word 'Acquire' or TWAIN Acquire. The scanning controls will be displayed.

Choosing the bit-depth

③ Choose 1-bit (line), 8-bit (grayscale) 24-bit (colour) or higher.

The bit-depth you choose will determine the mode of the scan and does not necessarily have to match the level of colour in the original.

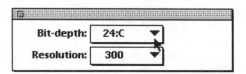

! Transmissive scanning programs have the additional option of selecting whether the subject is positive or negative. Choose whichever option is appropriate.

✚ Choosing a bit-depth usually alters the appearance of the pre-scanned image within the scanning controls window. See *Previewing the original*.

Choosing the resolution

④ Choose a resolution.

The resolution will be determined by the final use of the image. For all images destined for use in web pages, interactive presentations and multimedia projects, choose 72 ppi (dpi); for grayscale and colour images that will be printed, choose a resolution twice the proposed halftone screen; for line images that will be printed, choose a resolution of between 600 to 800 ppi (dpi).

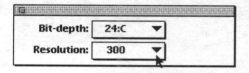

▲ Avoid using an interpolated resolution of more than twice the optical resolution, especially for line subjects.

✚ In some scanning programs, resolution is set by selecting a printer type, such as 'imagesetter'. This supposedly simpler method of resolution setting invariably limits the choice of resolution available to you.

Previewing the original

⑤ Click Preview, Prescan or an icon representing the command.

A quick scan will be made from the original.

❗ The colour of the pre-scanned image is usually determined by the current bit-depth setting. See step 3, *Choosing the bit-depth*.

Cropping the image

⑥ A dotted rectangle (cropping marquee) will be displayed over the pre-scanned image.
Move the pointer to one of its handles, or its edge (depending on your program).
Click-drag to resize the rectangle.

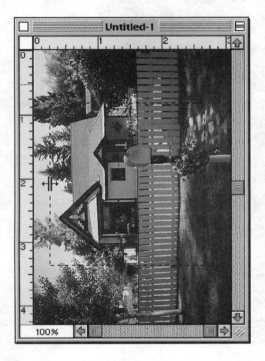

❗ If no cropping marquee is present, click-drag diagonally across the preview image with the pointer to create a marquee.

⑦ Move the pointer within the dotted rectangle. Click-drag to reposition the rectangle.

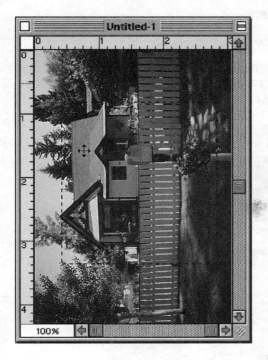

Setting the image dimensions

Either:

⑧ Enter a percentage value in the Scale field or click-drag the Scale slider.

Or:

⑧ Choose the unit of measurement, such as mm or pixels, and enter values in the Width and/or Height fields. Click to lock the Padlock icon beside the dimension field once you have entered a value. Some scanning controls have only one padlock for both dimensions.

▲ For images destined for interactive presentations and multimedia projects choose pixels as the measurement units.

Note that the value in the Scale field may change when you set a fixed dimension. This is quite normal and should not be altered.

The dotted rectangle indicating the crop may also change shape. You should readjust it by returning to steps 6 and 7.

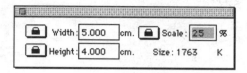

Checking the file size

⑨ Check the figure under File (or Image) Size. Either term refers to how much data will be contained in the scanned image. If you wish to reduce the size, reduce the resolution and/or dimensions of the image.

You may wish to do this so that the image occupies less space on a disk or within a host document. The latter consideration is particularly relevant for images destined for web pages and multimedia projects.

❗ Reducing the resolution is only an option for those images that will be printed. A resolution of one and a half times the halftone screen (instead of twice) will give reasonable quality.

Scanning the image

⑩ Click Scan.

The scanner will re-scan the original to your settings and automatically display the image within a Photoshop document window.

Rotating an image

If an original is presented sideways within the document window, rotate it.

● Choose an option in the Rotate Canvas sub-menu in the Image menu.

Saving a scan

Before you do any further work on your newly-scanned image, give it a name and save it to disk.

① Chose Save As... in the File menu. The Save As directory dialog box will be displayed.

② Enter a document name, overwriting the name Untitled-1.

③ Choose an option in the Format pop-up menu. If you are not sure which format to use, choose TIFF. The file format can always be altered later.

④ Select a drive and folder in which to save the file.

⑤ Click Save to save the document. Click Cancel if you wish to abort the routine.

The new name and mode will be shown in the document window title bar.

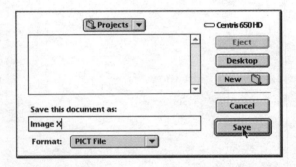

Once you are familiar with the scanning process and the controls on your particular scanner, move to Chapter 8, *Scanning accurately* for step-by-step instructions on how to get the best scans possible.

Summary:

● **Scanning is a method of capturing images in digitised form.**

● **The quality of originals has a direct effect on scan quality.**

● **Only scan at an over-high resolution and bit-depth when necessary.**

● **Key image attributes, which are set at the scanning stage, determine the amount of data in an image.**

5

VIEWING AND
RESIZING IMAGES

This chapter covers:

- file and image size indicators
- the Navigator palette
- the Cropping tool
- the Image Size dialog box
- the Canvas dialog box

Checking image attributes

Checking an image's attributes

You can check the dimensions, number of channels and resolution of an image without resorting to dialog boxes.

- Hold down ⎇ and press the Document Size panel at the bottom left of the document window. A pop-up panel will list the width, height, number of channels and resolution of an image.

You can also see how big an image is in relation to a printed page.

① Choose Page Setup in the File menu. Click A4 (for example) under Paper. Click OK.

② Hold down the mouse button with the pointer positioned over the Document size panel at the bottom left of document window. An A4 page preview will be displayed with a rectangle representing the image.

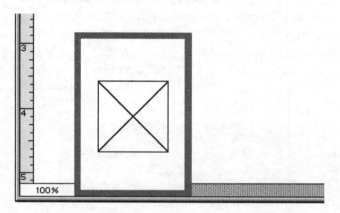

Checking an image's document size

It's important to be aware of an image's document size, if only to ensure you don't run up against memory problems. Some images, of necessity, will have a small file size, especially images destined for multimedia projects and web pages.

The document size is shown in a panel at the bottom left hand corner of the document window.

Checking the document size

● Choose Document sizes in the pop-up menu at the bottom left of the document window. The first figure indicates the final size of the document (without extra channels and layers). The second figure indicates the size of the document with extra channels and layers.

Viewing images

Viewing at different scales

Images can be viewed within Photoshop in a number of scales ranging from 0.13% to 1600%. When you view on an Actual Pixels basis (indicated as 100% in the document window title bar) one pixel on the screen represents one pixel in an image.

When you scale up or down, the relationship between the screen and image pixels alters, e.g. 400% indicates that 16 (4×4) pixels on the screen represent one pixel in the image; 25% indicates that one pixel on the screen represents 16 (4×4) pixels in the image.

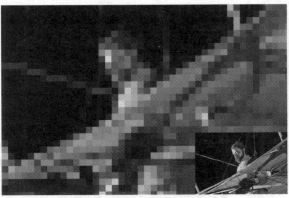

The same image viewed at two different scales.

Choosing Print Size enables you to view printed images at finished size on the screen, whatever their resolution. Choosing Actual Pixels enables you to view screen images at finished size, provided their resolution is 72 ppi.

In Photoshop 3.0, images can be viewed in one of nine scales each expressed as a ratio to the image resolution, e.g. 1:1 in the document window title bar indicates actual pixel basis and 16:1 indicates an enlargement of 1600%.

Unless you are working with images for multimedia projects, the scale ratio in which you happen to be working is academic. View at any scale which allows you to perform a given task with ease.

The viewing scale can be altered by using the View menu, by using the Zoom tool (with or without a modifier key), by keystrokes, by entering a percentage (%) value in the scale field in the document window or by means of Navigator palette (the two latter methods are available in Photoshop 4.0 only).

Viewing on a Actual Pixel basis

● double-click the Zoom tool.

Or:

● double-click the Hand tool. This also fits the document window to the image.

Or:

● choose Actual Pixels in the View menu (Photoshop 4.0 only).

Viewing on a Print Size basis

● Choose Print Size in the View menu (Photoshop 4.0 only).

Using the Zoom and keystrokes

① Select the Zoom tool (or hold down [⌘]+[Space]) and click or click-drag within the image to increase the viewing scale.

Hold down [Alt] (or hold down [Alt]+[Space]) and click within the image to reduce the viewing scale.

! The keyboard shortcut is the only way you can alter the scale when a dialog box is open.

② Reselect any other tool to deselect the Zoom tool (if selected from the tool palette).

Using the Navigator palette

Choose Show Navigator in the Window menu.

● Click the Zoom in and Zoom out icons or click-drag the Zoom Slider to alter the scale.

Or:

● enter a percentage (%) value in the bottom left scale field.

Or:

● click-drag the rectangle within the Proxy Preview Area to move around the image.

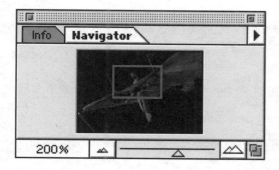

Viewing an image in two windows

① Open an image in the usual way.

② Choose New View in the View menu.

Moving around an image

You can move around an image using the scroll bars, the Hand tool and by means of Photoshop 4.0's Navigator palette.

Moving an image within the document window

● Use the scroll bars.

Or:

● select the Hand tool (or hold down [Space]) and click-drag the image.

Or:

● click-drag the rectangle within the Proxy Preview Area within the Navigator palette.

Hiding/displaying interface items

Windows, menu bars and palettes can be showing or hidden when you work.

Showing and hiding windows and menu bars

● Click one of the viewing modes at the screen modes at the bottom of the tool palette.

Showing and hiding all palettes

● Press [Tab]

Showing individual palettes

Either:

① choose Commands in the Window menu.

Click on palette name to show/hide individual palettes.

Or:

● choose a palette in the Window menu.

!   The Command palette is only available in Photoshop 3.0.

Positioning images

Rulers can be used to help you position pasted images within a document. The cursor position is tracked by a thin line within each ruler. In Photoshop 4.0, ruler guides can be added to documents to map out compositional areas.

Setting up the rulers

Showing and hiding rulers

● Choose Show Rulers in the View menu. If the rulers are already showing, the word 'Hide' will precede the command so there is no need to choose the command.

Altering the ruler units

The rulers can be calibrated in any one of five measurements units.

① Choose Units & Rulers... in the Preferences sub-menu in the File menu. The Units Preferences dialog box will be displayed.

② Choose an option in the Units pop-up menu.

③ Click OK.

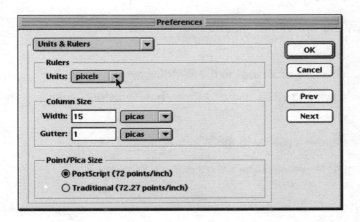

Moving the ruler zero points

You can measure from a point other than the top and left edges of an image. You do this by moving the ruler zero points.

① Click-drag from the small square at the junction of the rulers to a position within the document page.

② Release the mouse button. The zero points will have moved accordingly.

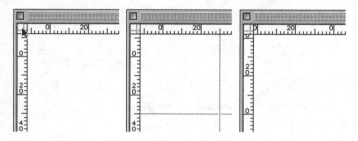

▲ Double-click within the same square to return the zero points to their original position.

Working with ruler guides

Adding a ruler guide

① Click-drag from somewhere in the middle of either ruler to a position within the image. Release the mouse button when you have reached the desired position.

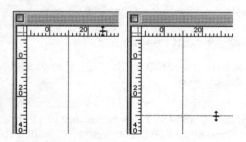

▲ Choose a viewing scale above 200% to position guides with greater accuracy. Hold down the Shift key when you click-drag to snap the guides to the ruler calibrations.

Moving a ruler guide

● Click-drag an existing guide using the Move tool.

Altering the orientation of ruler guide

● Hold down [Alt] and click guide.

Removing a single guide

● Click-drag the guide back to the ruler using the Move tool.

Removing all guides

● Choose Clear Guides in the View menu.

Locking all guides

● Choose Lock Guides in the View menu.

——————— Resizing images ———————

Altering the dimensions and resolution of an image

If you don't know the final dimensions and optimum resolution for an image when you are scanning, you can alter both attributes when you decide what they should be. In Photoshop 4.0, the control is split between print and multimedia attributes. For those working on screen images with Photoshop 3.0, follow the first set of steps only.

Altering the image size for print images

① Choose Image Size... in the Image menu. The Image size dialog box will be displayed.

② Check Constrain Proportions if you wish to maintain the image's current proportions. Uncheck Resample Image (or check File Size in Photoshop 3.0) if you wish to maintain the size of the file.

③ Enter new values in the dimension fields under Print Size (if Constrain Proportions is checked you only need to enter one value).

④ Enter a new value in the Resolution field under Print Size (if Resample Image is unchecked, any alteration will affect the dimensions). In Photoshop 3, if you don't wish to maintain the file size when altering the resolution, first choose a unit of measurement other than pixels for both dimensions and then enter a value in the Resolution field.

④ Note the revised amount in MB after Pixel Dimensions (after New Size in Photoshop 3), if the document size is important to you.

⑥ Click OK.

Altering the image size for screen images

① Choose Image Size... in the Image menu. The Image Size dialog box will be displayed.

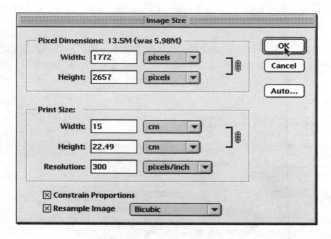

② Check Constrain Proportions if you wish to maintain the image's current proportions. Check Resample Image to allow the file size to be altered.

③ Enter new values in the fields under Pixel Dimensions (if Constrain Proportions is checked you only need to enter one value).

④ Note the revised amount in MB after Pixel Dimensions, if the document size is important to you.

⑤ Click OK.

If Resample Image is checked (File Size unchecked in the case of Photoshop 3.0) when the image size is altered, resampling usually takes place, resulting in pixels being added or deleted.

Increasing the pixel dimensions (file size) results in the creation of brand new pixels based on existing tonal/colour values. Large increases in size, four times the current size and upwards, leads to dithering on the edges of images, obvious pixelation, lack of sharpness and loss of detail.

Reducing the pixel dimensions (file size) results in the removal of pixels. Extreme reductions have no detrimental visual effects, provided the resolution is appropriate for a given use.

Any resampling involves interpolation, a process of assigning colours to pixels. The method of interpolation can be altered to suit a particular image. Bicubic gives the best quality; Nearest Neighbour retains sharp edges within images and is appropriate for certain graphic subjects.

In Photoshop 4.0, the method is chosen within the pop-up menu at the bottom of the Image Size dialog box. In Photoshop 3.0 the method is chosen within the General Preferences dialog box.

Recropping an image

Recropping an image freely

①   Select the Cropping tool.

②   Uncheck Fixed Target Size in the Cropping Tool Options palette.

③   Click-drag diagonally across an image to define the crop area.

④   Select the Move tool to implement the cropping. An alert box saying 'Crop the Image?' will be displayed.

⑤   Click Crop or Cancel.

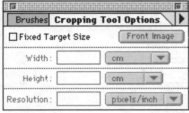

❗   In Photoshop 3.0 instead of selecting the Move tool, click within the cropping border to implement the crop.

✚   Cropping freely reduces the dimensions of an image whilst maintaining its resolution. No resampling takes place when the tool is used in this way.

Constraining a crop and/or altering the resolution

①   Select the Crop tool.

②   Check Fixed Target Size in the Cropping Tool Options palette.

③   Enter values in the Width and/or Height fields. Choose the unit of measurement you wish to use in the adjacent pop-up menus. If you do not wish to fix one of the dimensions, leave its field blank.

④   Optionally, enter a value in the Resolution field. Choose the unit of measurement you wish to use in the adjacent pop-up menu. If you do not wish to change the resolution, leave this field blank.

⑤   Click-drag diagonally across an image to define the crop area. A cropping border will be displayed.

⑥   Move the pointer to one of the handles of the crop border and click-drag to re-adjust a crop.

⑦   Move the pointer to the edge of the crop border (but away from any one handle) and click-drag to rotate a crop.

⑧   Select the Move tool to implement the crop. An alert box saying 'Crop the Image?' will be displayed.

⑨   Click Crop or Cancel.

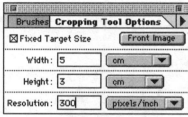

!   In Photoshop 3.0 to move the cropping border, hold down the Command key and click-drag a handle. To rotate the cropping border, hold down the Alt key instead.

✛   Entering a resolution results in the resampling of the cropped area, resulting in the creation or removal of pixels. See *Resizing images* (pages 40–43).

Creating extra working area

You can create extra space around an image to give you more working area. This function is especially useful when composing montages.

①   Select a current Background colour. This colour will be used for the extended space.

②   Choose Canvas Size... in the Image menu. The Canvas Size dialog box will be displayed.

③   Enter values in the Width and Height fields.

④ In the grid at the bottom of the dialog box, click where you wish the existing image to be in relation to the extra space.

⑤ Click OK.

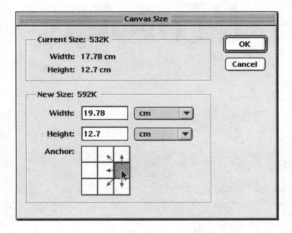

Summary:

● You can view at any scale which allows you to perform a given task with ease.

● You can alter the dimensions and/or resolution of an image using the Image Size controls.

● Increasing the file size by more than 400%, when resizing, often leads to poor image quality.

● You can crop an image freely or fix a target size.

● Cropping freely avoids any image resampling.

6

USING COLOURS

This chapter covers:

- the Tool palette
- the Swatches palette
- the Picker palette
- the Scratch palette
- the Colour Picker dialog box
- the Custom Colours dialog box

—————— Choosing colours ——————

The concept of current colours

Whilst over 16.7 million colours are available to you within Photoshop, only two colours are current at any one time: one is the foreground colour for painting, filling and stroking selections and one is the background colour. The painting tools use the current foreground colour; the eraser tool exposes the current background colour.

In addition, the current background colour is used to extend the image's overall dimensions – its canvas – and for blending gradients.

Since the two colours can be any hue you wish and can be constantly altered as you work, this does not limit your colouring work in any way.

✦ Only black and white are available in line images, whilst 256 shades of grey are available in grayscale images.

—— Altering current colours ——

Current colours can be altered in one of five ways:

● by sampling coloured pixels from your image or from colour swatches

● by mixing red, green and blue in various proportions

● by mixing colours using the painting tools

● by using the Photoshop Colour Picker

● by choosing Pantone colours.

Whichever method you use to alter the colours, they are always displayed as overlapping swatches in the Tool and Colour palettes.

The default colours are black (foreground) and white (background).

It is via these overlapping swatches that the Photoshop Colour Picker is accessed and – more importantly – the Pantone colours.

Otherwise all colours are sampled from pixels within the scanned image, from colour swatches or from paint mixes, or by specifying RGB (red, green and blue) colours.

❗ In Photoshop 3.0 the Colour palette is called the Picker palette.

Sampling colours

Sampling your image

❶ Select the Eyedropper tool in the tool palette.

❷ Click on a colour pixel in your image to alter the foreground colour (hold down [Alt] to alter the background colour).

▲ Alter the Eyedropper tool's sampling area for broader colour sampling. Choose a 3 by 3 average or 5 by 5 average in the Sample Size menu in the Options palette.

Sampling a swatch

❶ Position the cursor over a colour swatch in the Swatches palette (hold down [Alt] to alter the background colour). The cursor turns into the eyedropper tool.

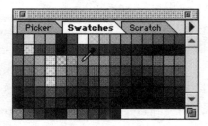

❷ Click the mouse button.

Mixing RGB colours

Using the Colour palette (Picker palette in Photoshop 3.0)

❶ Select Colour in the Window menu. Click once on the upper (foreground) colour swatch or lower (background) colour swatch at the top right of the palette (if the swatch it is already outlined, there is no need to click).

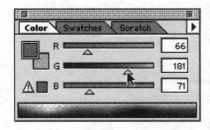

❷ Click a colour within the colour bar on lower part of palette or click-drag the RGB sliders.

▲   If a small triangle is displayed within the palette, the colour you have selected is 'out-of-gamut'. If you wish to bring the colour within the CMYK gamut, click the triangle.

You can mix colours using colours from another style (mode) within the Colour palette. The colour style (mode) in the Colour palette defaults to the mode of your image. So if you wish to mix CMYK colours within an RGB image, choose CMYK in the Colour palette's menu.

Mixing paint colours

The Scratch palette is a useful place to experiment with different colour blends. The main paint tools are at your disposal within the palette and you can change your view using the Zoom and Hand tools. Remember, when overlaying colours, always reduce the opacity of your tool so that colours blend to form new colours and don't just obliterate one another.

Using the Scratch palette

① Choose Scratch and Options in turn in the Window menu.

② Select White as the Background colour.

③ Choose Clear in the Scratch palette menu to clear the palette of existing colours.

④ Select a painting tool in the Tool palette.

⑤ Paint directly onto the Scratch palette.

⑥ Alter the current foreground colour by using one of the methods described previously.

⑦ Within the Options palette, reset the tool opacity to less than 100%.

⑧ Paint over the original paint mark.

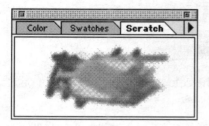

⑧ Continue the process until you have created the desired colour.

⑨ Select the Eyedropper tool and click on the colour.

▲ If you are creating lots of mixes using the Scratch palette in conjunction with the Colour and Swatches palettes, you may find it more convenient to separate the Scratch palette from the other palettes. Do this by click-dragging the tabbed area of the palette away from the others.

Using a colour picker

Using the Photoshop Picker

① Double-click either the foreground or background colour icons on the Tool or Colour palette.

② Click-drag the vertical slider within the Colour Picker.

③ Click on the colour area to the left. Click OK.

✦ The Apple Colour Picker can be used instead of the Photoshop Picker for choosing colours but is is not as versatile as the Photoshop Picker. Choose Apple in the Colour Picker menu in the General Preferences dialog box.

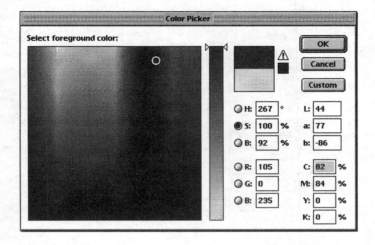

! Alert icons in the Colour palette and Photoshop Colour Picker warn you that your chosen colour is 'out-of-gamut' and therefore cannot be reproduced accurately using the standard process (CMYK) printing colours. If you are choosing colours for multimedia work, this warning can be ignored. However, if you are planning to print your image in any way, click on the alert icon to choose the closest reproduceable colour. This colour may be quite a bit different from your preferred colour but you can be certain it will be faithfully reproduced.

Using Pantone colours

Selecting a Pantone colour

① Double-click either the foreground or background colour icons on the Tool or Colour palette.

② Click Custom in the Colour Picker.

③ Choose Pantone Coated or Pantone Uncoated in the Book pop-up menu.

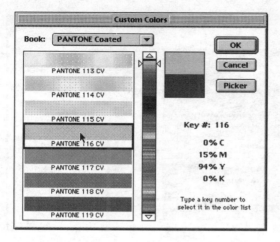

④ Select a Pantone colour by:

Either: click-dragging the triangles along the scroll bar and then clicking a colour swatch.

Or: typing the Pantone reference number using the keyboard.

⑤ Click OK.

✚ More than one Pantone type is listed in the Book pop-up menu in the Custom dialog box. Choose Pantone Coated for images to be printed on smooth surface printing papers, such as gloss and matt finish art papers, and choose Pantone Uncoated for images to be printed on rough surface printing papers, such as cartridge and stationery papers.

Swapping and reverting colours

Swopping the current colours

● Click on the Switch colours icon (double-ended arrows) at the top right of the overlapping swatches on the Tools palette.

Reverting to the default current colours

● Click on the Default colours icon at the bottom left of the overlapping swatches on the tools palette.

Saving colours

Creating your own palette of swatches

Adding the current colours to the Swatches palette

① Alter the foreground or background colour to select a colour you wish to add.

② Hold down [Shift] to replace a swatch with a new colour ([Alt]+[Shift] to add a new colour). The cursor turns into the Paint bucket tool.

③ Click the mouse button.

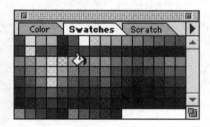

Removing colours from the Swatches palette

① Hold down [⌘]

② Click the mouse button.

▲ Use the Scratch palette to experiment with colour blends of your own.

Seeing how the colours are applied

① Choose a Foreground and a Background colour.

② Select the Paint brush tool within the Tool palette.

③ In the Paint Brush Options palette, adjust the opacity to, say, 50%. In the Brushes palette select a suitable tip size.

④ Paint over part of the image. Notice how the paint colour blends with the image.

⑤ Select the Eraser tool within the Tool palette. In the Brushes palette select a suitable tip size.

⑥ Erase part of the image. Notice how it removes the image, 'exposing' the background colour.

Summary:

- You use the current foreground colour for painting, filling and stroking work.

- You expose the background colour with the eraser.

- You can change the current colours in many ways and using different colour styles (or modes).

- You can access Pantone colours from within the Photoshop Colour Picker.

- You can save colours of your choice in the Swatches palette to ensure colour consistency and speed of working.

7

SELECTING AREAS AND FILLING

This chapter covers:

- the Marquee, Lasso and Magic Wand tools
- the Options palette
- the Select menu
- the Quick Mask mode
- the Channels palette
- the Fill dialog box
- the Paint Bucket and Gradient tools

Selection tools isolate areas of an image for subsequent treatment. They do this by temporarily masking off areas which you don't wish to alter.

There is a formidable range of selection tools and commands within Photoshop. Each isolates areas in different ways. Used in combination, any range of pixels can be selected, given time and patience.

Once areas are selected, they can be cut and copied, moved, filled, transformed, filtered and colour-corrected. Apart from filling, these further processes are covered in other sections.

—— Basic selection methods ——

Selecting simple areas

You can select rectangular and elliptical areas using the Marquee tool.

①   Select the Marquee tool. If the version of the Marquee tool you wish to use is not displayed in the Tool palette, hold down [Alt] and click the Marquee tool. Alternatively choose the alternative version in the Marquee Options palette.

②   Click-drag diagonally within the image. Hold down [Alt] to centre the selection at the point from which you drag.

▲   Choose Constrained Aspect Ratio in the Style pop-up menu in the Marquee Options palette to select areas to a set proportion.

Selecting free form areas

①   Select the Lasso tool.

②   Either: click-drag a shape within the image.

    Or: hold down [Alt] [Shift] and click at different points within the image to create straight border edges.

Either way there is no need for you to complete the shape fully. Photoshop will do this automatically for you.

!   In Photoshop 3.0 only hold down the Alt key to create straight border edges.

▲   Give a feather edge to selections by entering a value in the Feather field in the Marquee and Lasso Options palettes.

Give a soft edge to selections by checking Anti-Aliased in the Marquee and Lasso Options palettes.

—— Further selection methods ——

Selecting non-selected parts of an image

●   Choose Inverse in the Select menu.

Selecting and deselecting all areas

Selecting an entire image

●   Choose All in the Select menu.

Deselecting all selections within an image

Either:

● click somewhere on the image with any selection tool (except the Magic Wand tool).

Or:

● choose None in the Select menu.

Selecting areas through colour similarity

Sometimes you will need to select flattish regions within an image, such as areas of sky or plain interior walls. Whilst it would be possible for you to use the Lasso tool to select such areas, it could take you a great deal of time and requires excellent hand/eye co-ordination to do an accurate job, especially if the areas are expansive and have untidy edges.

Fortunately these areas can be selected on the basis of colour instead of shape. The tool which performs this task is the Magic Wand and its tolerance level (sensitivity) is adjustable from 0 to 255.

When you click on a pixel, the tool will select all abutting pixels within its tolerance range, but not isolated pixels.

Selecting pixels within a similar tonal/colour range

① Select the Magic Wand tool.

② Enter a value in the range 0–255 in the Tolerance field in the Magic Wand Options palette.

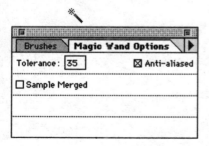

③　Check the Anti-aliased box.

④　Click within the area of the image you wish to select.

▲　Check the Anti-Aliased box in the Magic Wand Options palette to give a soft edge to selections; uncheck the Anti-aliased box to give a hard edge.

✚　A low tolerance value, of say 20, will select contiguous areas containing pixels with values that are up to 10 on either side of the selected pixel value. Higher values select image areas containing a wider range of colours; 255 will select everything.

Seeing how the selection borders work

①　Select the Marquee tool within the Tool palette. Within the Marquee Options palette, select Rectangular in the Shape pop-up menu and Normal in the Style pop-up menu.

②　Select an area of the image.

③　Select the Paint brush tool in the Tool palette.

④　In the Paint Brush Options palette, adjust the opacity to, say, 50%. In the Brushes palette select a suitable tip size. See *The brushes palette* (page 9).

⑤　Paint right across the border of the selected area. Notice how the area within the selection border is painted and the area outside the border is untouched.

—— Further selection methods ——

Extending and reducing selections

Adding to a selection

- Hold down [Shift] and select the area you wish to add to the current selection(s).

Subtracting from a selection

- Hold down [Alt] and select the area you wish to subtract from current selection(s).

! In Photoshop 3.0 hold down the Command key instead.

Selecting parts of two selections

- Select either the Marquee or Lasso tool, hold down [Alt] [Shift] and create the area by overlapping two previously selected areas.

! In Photoshop 3.0 hold down the Command and Shift keys instead.

Giving selections a feathered edge

You can give selection borders a feathered edge. If you then fill the selection, a smooth transition will be created between the fill and any bordering tones/colours. Alternatively, if you inverse the feathered selection, the image can be vignetted (given a soft edge).

① Choose Feather…in the Select menu. The Feather Selection dialog box will be displayed.

② Enter an amount in the Feather Radius… pixels field.

③ Click OK.

④ Either: fill the selection.

Or: choose Inverse in the Select menu and press [Delete]

✦ In Photoshop 4.0 a floating selection is a selection which has been moved or copied without using the Clipboard but has yet to be deselected. In Photoshop 3.0 moving or copying a selection using the Clipboard also results in a floating selection.

Extending selections through colour

You can extend an existing selection based on colour similarity using the Grow and Similar commands.

The Grow command extends the selection to pixels adjacent to a selection. The Similar command extends the selection to all pixels within an image. Both commands are controlled by the current Magic Wand tolerance setting.

Extending selections through colour

①   Enter a tolerance value in the Magic Wand Options palette.

②   Choose Grow or Similar in the Select menu.

Adjusting selections using the paint tools

You may find it easier to add to or subtract from selections using the paint tools. In Quick Mask mode, unselected (masked) areas are represented by a reddish tint instead of an animated selection border. You can use the paint tools to paint areas in or paint areas out, to soften their edges and generally to clean things up.

After you have made any alterations to the mask, you then revert the image back to Standard mode.

①   Make a selection in the normal way.

② Click on the Quick Mask icon in the Tools palette. Unselected areas will automatically be tinted a reddish colour.

③ Use the painting tools to retouch the tinted areas. This work does not affect the image itself, but only the mask.

④ When you've finished, reselect the Standard Mode icon in the tool palette.

▲ You can change the Quick Mask tint colour or switch the tint to the selected areas. To do either, double click on the Quick Mask icon. The Quick Mask Options dialog box will be displayed. Click Selected Areas. Click the colour swatch if you wish to change the reddish tint to another colour. Click OK.

Moving a selection border

You can move a selection border without moving its contents.

● With any of the selection tools active, click-drag the selection border.

❗ In Photoshop 3.0 hold down the Command and Alt keys.

Moving and duplicating selections

Moving selected areas

① Select the Move tool (or if you have another tool selected, hold down [⌘]).

② Click-drag the selection border. The selection moves with the current background colour taking its place.

Duplicating selected areas

① Select the Move tool (or if you have another tool selected, hold down ⌘).

② Hold down Alt and click-drag the selection border. A duplicate of the selection moves leaving the original in place.

! In Photoshop 3.0 hold down the Alt key and click-drag with the Marquee or Lasso tool.

▲ Move a selection/selection area a pixel at a time by using the arrow keys on the keyboard.

Constrain the movement of selections to 45°, by holding down the Shift key whilst you click-drag.

Saving selections for later use

You can save selections to use them later or as a precaution against losing a selection in error.

Saving an active selection

① Choose Save Selection… in the Select menu. The Save Selection dialog box will be displayed.

② Click OK.

③ Choose None in the Select menu if you wish to deselect the current selection.

! Each saved selection adds another channel to a document. When you have finished with a selection, remove the channel to reduce the file size of your document.

Reloading a saved selection

① Choose Load Selection… in the Select menu. The Load Selection dialog box will be displayed.

② Choose the selection in the Channel pop-up menu.

③ Click OK.

Removing a saved selection

①   Choose Channels… in the Palettes sub-menu in the Window menu. The Channels palette will be displayed.

②   Click on the channel containing the selection.

③   Choose Delete Channel in the Channels palette pop-up menu.

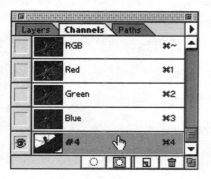

Filling selections

Filling selections with flat colour

Filling selections with the current foreground colour

Either:

①   choose Fill… in the Edit menu. The Fill dialog box will be displayed.

②   Choose a current colour in the Colour pop-up menu.

③   Enter a value in the Opacity box. Select the Mode.

④   Click OK.

Or:

●   press ⟨Alt⟩ + ⟨Delete⟩

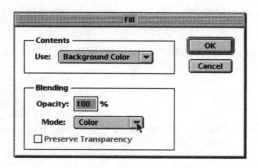

! The latter method ignores the current settings in the Fill dialog box.

Filling non-floating selections with the background colour.

Either:

● choose Clear in the Edit menu.

Or:

● press [Delete]

Filling pixels within a colour range

Painting an area using the paint bucket

① Select the Paint Bucket tool.

② Enter a value in the Tolerance box in the Paint Bucket Options palette. Check Anti-aliased if you wish the edge of the filled area to be softened.

③ Click on area of image.

▲ Enter a low value to fill pixels within a narrow tonal/colour range. Enter a high value to fill pixels within a broader tonal/colour range.

Filling selections with graduated colour

① Select the part of the image you wish to fill.

② Select the Gradient tool.

③ Choose Linear or Radial blend in the Type pop-up menu in the Gradient Tool Options palette.

④ Choose an option in the Gradient pop-up menu in the same palette.

⑤ Position the pointer to where you wish the foreground colour to start graduating.

⑥ Click-drag to define the direction, length or radius of the gradient.

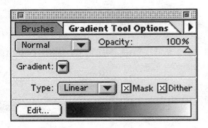

Summary:

● **Use the selection tools to isolate areas of an image for subsequent treatment.**

● **Save complicated selections borders in case you deselect them by mistake or if you wish to use them at a later date.**

● **Alter selection borders using the paint tools in Quick Mask mode.**

● **Fill selection borders by using the Fill command or Gradient tool.**

● **Copy and paste feathered selections to give images vignetted edges.**

8

SCANNING
ACCURATELY

This chapter covers:

● scanning controls
● the Save As directory dialog box

Scanning approaches

Obtaining good scans from originals depends on setting the correct mode, resolution, and dimensional settings for a given subject.

The mode is usually determined by the level of colour you wish to have in a final image, but this is not always so; image dimensions depend on the size at which you wish to use an image and resolution depends on outputting or retouching factors.

Continuous tone and line subjects demand different scanning approaches, depending on the bit-depth you require.

For continuous tone subjects, the critical settings are resolution and dimensions. Resolution is always based on either halftone or monitor screen resolution and dimensions on final image size.

Graphic motifs, such as colour logotypes and symbols, are a special case. The resolution needs to be much higher than the level you finally plan to use so that you can more easily re-establish their design properties through retouching.

For line subjects, the critical settings are resolution, dimensions and mode. Since 1-bit images tend to break up edges and reduce linear detail, resolution needs to be as high as possible, but no more than twice your scanner's optical resolution. So that you can tonally adjust and rotate images, the mode needs to be grayscale.

Scanning is an acquired skill. Getting good results from originals, whatever the subject, often involves much trial and error.

Follow the steps in this chapter a number of times with different originals to develop your expertise but don't be too disappointed if your initial scans don't immediately match up to your expectations. It takes time, experience and confidence to reach a position where you can get them right first time.

As you follow the steps, refer to *The scanning process* covered in Chapter 4, for basic information on how to use the controls.

Close-up of a line subject in grayscale

Halftones and resolution

Continuous tone (grayscale and colour) images, by definition, contain graduations and are therefore 'halftoned' when output to print.

Halftoning is a process of converting tonal and colour values to a screen of dots of varying sizes. The varying sized dots are usually small enough for the eye to merge them together to give a sensation of tonal and colour variety.

Halftoning is necessary because the most widely used printing technologies are not intrinsically tonal, i.e. areas of their printing surfaces are either fully inked or free from ink – there's no in-between.

Halftone screens are measured in lines per inch (lpi) and can be as low as 60 lpi, for grayscale images in newspapers, or as high as 200 lpi for colour images in art books.

The resolution of a contone (continuous tone) image needs to be roughly twice the proposed halftone screen, e.g. an image which will be screened at 120 lpi needs to have a resolution of 240 ppi (dpi).

Close-up of a halftone screen

Your printing company will be able to advise you on the halftone screen they plan to use for your images.

If you are solely outputting on a desktop printer, base the resolution on the default halftone screen values used by the printer. Normally this will be around a fifth of the printer resolution.

In the case of images for web pages, interactive presentations and multimedia projects, the resolution needs to be set at 72 ppi. This resolution is based not on any halftone screen – since no halftone is involved with screen display – but on Apple's multimedia standard for monitor screen resolution.

Those new to scanning are often surprised by the low resolution required for contone images compared with the higher resolution required for line images. Suffice to say that the halftone dots which define continuous tone images are much larger and less numerous than the imageset dots which define line images, and therefore require less data to describe them.

▲　Since die-sublimation printers don't employ a halftone screen, base the resolution on a fifth of the device's resolution.

✦　Halftone dots are sometimes called superpixels as they are formed by clusters of imageset dots.

Scanning tonal images

Scanning steps

Refer to *The scanning process* in Chapter 4 for operational information on each step.

Scanning the image

① Insert the original.

② Acquire the scanning program.

③ Preview the original.

④ Crop and set the dimensions of the image, based roughly on the largest size at which you are going to use the image.

⑤ Choose either grayscale or colour.

⑥ Set the resolution at twice the halftone screen or, in the case of multimedia images, at 72 ppi.

⑦ Check the image size: alter settings if necessary.

⑧ Choose a De-screen option (if available), if the original has been printed.

⑨ Scan the image and save the image in TIFF format.

⑩   Refine crop to finished dimensions maintaining resolution, rotating if necessary, using the Crop tool at Fixed Target Size.

▲   For multimedia images, set the dimensions accurately in pixels.

✦   A De-screen setting will minimise the halftone screen, if present within a subject.

Recropping the image

⑪   Re-crop the image, rotating if necessary.

Adjusting contrast

⑫   Choose Levels... in the Adjust sub-menu in the Image menu. The Levels dialog box will be displayed.

⑬   Clicking the Auto icon to create good black and white points. Only do this if you wish the darkest tone to be black and the lightest tone to be white.

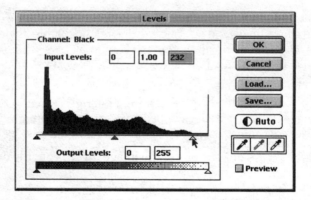

⑭   Click-drag inward the left and right triangles in the upper control until the the image looks correct.

⑮   Click OK.

⑯   Re-save.

    The image is now ready for further image improvement.

──────── Scanning line images ────────

Line illustrations, maps, plans, type and artwork present a special challenge to those involve in scanning. Edges in line subjects need to be sharp whatever their angle. Line scans break everything up into a 'mosaic' of bits and when edges are neither vertical or horizontal they are aliased (stepped).

A line image therefore needs to be of a high enough resolution for the average eye not to notice its stepped edges, but not so high that it creates overlarge file sizes. Furthermore, linear detail in subjects often needs faithfully to match originals. Line scans always remove any subtle darks and lights, resulting in loss of detail.

Images therefore need to be scanned in grayscale to give you control over how these tones are converted.

Once adjustments have been made, they can then be converted to Bitmap mode should you wish to create 1-bit images for use in DTP documents.

✦   Unlike contone images, line images, by definition, have no tonal graduation and are therefore not 'halftoned' when output. The dots which make up the final printed image are the very same dots that an outputting device uses to print the typematter, ranging from 300 dpi on a desktop printer to 2540 dpi on an imagesetter.

Scanning steps

Refer to *The scanning process* in Chapter 4 for operational information on each step.

Scanning the image

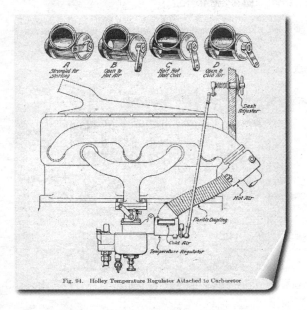

Fig. 94. Holley Temperature Regulator Attached to Carburetor

①   Insert an original. Place it accurately on the scanner glass, with the image square to the edges.

▲   Attach small originals to A4 sheets of paper. Use a set square to ensure an image is square to the edges of a sheet and use low adhesive clear tape as a fixing material if you wish to avoid damaging originals in any way. Align the edge of the sheet to the rulers on the glass and your image should be square to the scanner.

②   Load the scanning program.

③   Preview the original.

④   Loosely crop and set the dimensions of the image, based roughly on the largest size at which you are going to use the image.

⑤   Choose the 8-bit, grayscale mode.

⑥   Set the resolution at 600 or 800 ppi (dpi).

⑦   Check the image size.

⑧   Scan the image.

⑨   Save the image in TIFF format.

❗   The resolution should be no more than twice your scanner's optical resolution.

▲   For multimedia images, set the dimensions accurately in pixels.

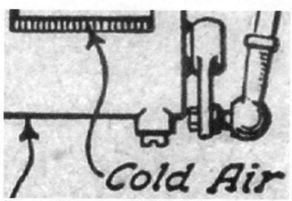

Close-up of the line diagram showing grey values

Recropping the image

●   Re-crop the image, rotating if necessary.

   If the image was scanned at lower than 600 ppi, check the Fixed Target Size box in the Cropping Tool Options palette and enter 600 in the Resolution field before using the tool.

Adjusting contrast

①   Choose Levels... in the Adjust sub-menu in the Image menu. The Levels dialog box will be displayed.

②   Click the Auto icon to create good black and white points.

③   Click-drag inward the left and right triangles in the upper control to restrict the grey levels to mostly black and white.

④ Click-drag the centre triangle in the upper control to improve the detail in the blacks and whites.

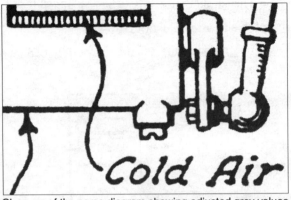

Close-up of the same diagram showing adjusted grey values

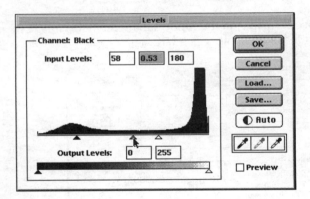

Further steps

Either:

● Reduce the resolution to production levels if you wish to maintain the image as a high contrast grayscale file. Such files are particularly suitable for images destined for web pages and multimedia projects.

Or:

① Choose Threshold... in the Adjust sub-menu of the Image menu. The Threshold dialog box will be displayed.

② Click-drag the slider to adjust the threshold.

③ Click OK. The grayscale file will now have only two levels of grey.

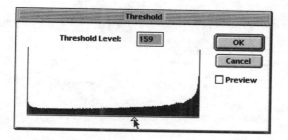

④ Choose Bitmap... in the Mode sub-menu in the Image menu. Select 50% Threshold. Click OK.

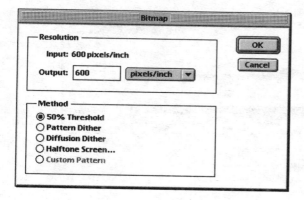

⑤ Re-save.

▲ Save Bitmap images in EPS format if you wish to have transparent whites.

If you are saving an image to a floppy disk and you need to reduce its file size without altering either its resolution or dimensions, resave the image in TIFF format, selecting LZW Compression within the TIFF Options dialog box.

——— Scanning colour logos ———

Colour logotypes and other graphic devices are, in many ways, more difficult subjects than line originals. Image sharpness, the maintainance of fine detail, colour accuracy – all are essential for faithful reproduction.

These properties are always more easy reproduced by scanning good originals, i.e. master images which are large, sharp and accurate in every detail. Such masters can be supplied by the design consultancies who provide corporate identity services to companies.

In the absence of good masters you can always scan images from corporate letterheads and marketing material; these are often more readily available but bear in mind that the poorer the original, the more retouching work will be involved and the final result may still not satisfy you.

Scanning steps

Refer to Chapter 4, *The scanning process* for operational information on each step and Chapter 9, *Retouching images* for how to re-establish design attributes in scans.

Scanning the image

①   Insert an original. Place it accurately on the scanner glass, with the logotype square to the edges.

▲   Attach small originals to A4 sheets of paper. Use a setsquare to ensure an image is square to the edges of a sheet and use low-adhesive clear tape as a fixing material. Butt the edge of the sheet to the rulers at the edge of the glass and your image should be square to the scanner.

② Load the scanning program.

③ Preview the original.

④ Loosely crop and set the dimensions of the image, based on the largest final size.

⑤ Choose the 24-bit colour mode.

⑥ Set the resolution at 800 ppi.

⑦ Check the image size.

⑧ Scan the image.

⑨ Save the image in TIFF format.

Close-up of scanned logotype showing tonal values.

❗ If the image was scanned at lower than 800 ppi, enter 800 in the Resolution field in the Cropping tool options palette and check the Fixed target size box before using the tool.

Cropping the image

⑩ Re-crop the image, straightening if necessary.

Adjusting contrast

⑫ Choose Levels... in the Adjust sub-menu in the Image menu. The Levels dialog box will be displayed.

⑬ Click the Auto icon to create good black and white points. Only do this if there is white and black in the subject.

⑭ Click-drag inward the left and right triangles in the upper control until the tonal contrast matches the original logotype.

⑮ Click OK.

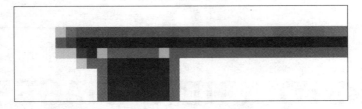

Close-up of the same scan showing corrected tonal values.

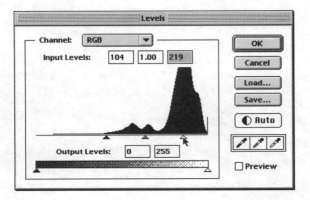

See *Retouching colour logotypes* (page 88) for how to re-establish design properties in scans.

Summary:

- **Scan continuous tone subjects at final resolutions to finished dimensions.**

- **Scan line subjects in grayscale at a high resolution and change the mode and resolution after making tonal adjustments.**

- **Scan colour logotypes at a high resolution and change the resolution after re-establishing design attributes.**

9

RETOUCHING IMAGES

This chapter covers:

- the Dust and Scratches filter
- the Focus tools
- the Toning tools
- the Eraser and Smudge tools
- the Rubber Stamp tool
- the Snapshot Command

Reasons for retouching

Most scanned images require some minor editing and retouching work before they are ready to be used in documents. Defects, scratches, scuffs, and crease marks on originals; blemishes and other unwanted details in subjects: all of these imperfections may be present in images, and they will need to be removed.

Retouching generally

Removing dust marks and scratches

①   Choose Dust and Scratches... in the Noise sub-menu in the Filter menu. The Dust & Scratches dialog box will be displayed.

②   Click on a dusty or scratched area of the image in document window. The area will then automatically show in the dialog box window.

③   Click on + or – to enlarge or reduce the preview image.

④   Drag the Threshold slider to the left until it reads zero.

⑤   Drag the Radius slider left or right until the defect disappears. Keep to the smallest radius possible.

⑥   Increase the Threshold to the highest amount possible without re-displaying the defects.

⑦   Click OK.

Blurring/sharpening an image area

Blurring/sharpening part of an image

① Select the Blur or Sharpen tool. If the focus tool you wish to use is not displayed in the Tool palette, choose the other tool in the pop-up menu in the Focus Tools Options palette.

② Choose a tonal range in the pop-up menu in the Focus Tools Options palette.

③ Click-drag. Blur will progressively soften an area. Sharpen will give more definition to an area.

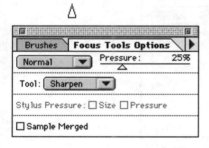

▲ The tendency is to over-apply the focus tools so always choose an appropriately-sized brush in the Brushes palette and set a low pressure, such as 20, in the Focus Tools Options palette.

Select Brush Size in the Display and Cursor Preferences dialog box to see the editing area of the brush you have selected.

Lightening/darkening an image area

Dodging and 'printing in' part of an image

① Select the Dodge or Burn tool. If the toning tool you wish to use is not displayed in the Tool palette, choose the other tool in the pop-up menu in the Toning Tools Options palette.

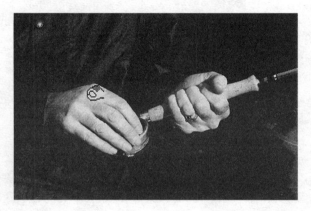

② Click-drag. Dodge will progressively lighten an area. Burn will progressively darken an area.

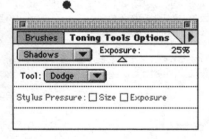

▲ The tendency is to over-apply the toning tools so always choose an appropriately-sized brush in the Brushes palette and set a low exposure, such as 20, in the Toning Tools Options palette.

Select Brush Size in the Display and Cursor Preferences dialog box to see the editing area of the brush you have selected.

Altering the saturation an image

Sometimes areas within an image lack sufficient colour (are under-saturated) or have too much colour (are over-saturated).

Over-saturation is not necessarily a problem for images restricted to being displayed on screen. However it may be a problem if an image is to be printed because over-saturated areas won't reproduce accurately. This is because printing devices have a different gamut (range of colours) from monitor screens.

Under-saturation is usually a subjective consideration, whatever the media concerned.

To help you identify over-saturated areas, exclamation marks appear after the CMYK values in the Info palette when you pass the cursor over such areas. Additionally, a gamut alert triangle appears in both the Colour palette and Colour Picker if you select an over-saturated foreground or background colour.

Over-saturated areas within images are also identified as grey pixels within the Gamut Warning mode. Over-saturated (out-of-gamut) colours can be brought within gamut by using the Sponge tool. This method allows you to alter the saturation locally on images where colour accuracy is of paramount importance.

Alternatively you can let Photoshop automatically bring colours into gamut for you when you change the mode of an image from RGB to CMYK. See *Preparing images for print* (page 146).

✚　Saturation is the extent to which colours are dulled or greyed. When you adjust the colour control on your television, you are effectively adjusting colour saturation.

Altering saturation locally

When you use the Sponge tool, it's best to have two document windows open, each in a different mode.

Displaying out-of-gamut colours (window 1).

①　Choose Gamut Warning in the View menu. Out-of-gamut colours will show as grey.

Opening a second document window (window 2).

②   Choose New View in the Window menu.

③   Choose CMYK Preview in the View menu. The preview simulates how the RGB image will look in CMYK.

!   The correct calibration and separation settings in the Printing Inks Setup and Separation Setup dialog boxes must be in place for the above preview to be accurate.

Tiling the document windows

④   Size and position both windows so they can be viewed together.

Working with the Sponge tool in the window 1.

⑤   Select the Sponge tool.

⑥   Select a large, soft edged brush in the Toning Tools Brushes palette.

⑦   Choose Desaturate and 20-30% pressure in the Toning Tools Options palette.

⑧   Click-drag over offending areas. Colours will be progressively desaturated, removing the grey tinted areas as the colours fall into gamut. View window 2 to check that you are not under saturating the image too much.

⑨   Choose Gamut Warning in the View menu to untick this command.

⑩   Close window 2.

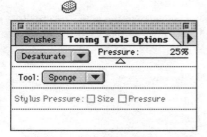

▲   Select Brush Size in the Display and Cursor Preferences dialog box to see the editing area the brush you have selected.

Erasing parts of an image

Erasing pixels within an image

①   Select the Eraser tool.

②   Click-drag. Erased areas expose the current background colour.

▲   Use the Eraser as an alternative to the Paint, Pencil and Airbrush tools. Choose an option in the mode pop-up menu in the Eraser Tool Options palette and paint with the current background colour.

Smudging an image area

①   Select the Smudge tool.

②   Click-drag. The tool will smudge an area by pushing image colour in the direction of the drag.

Retouching an image area by cloning

Sometimes you will wish to remove defects within an image, such as litter on a pavement or a mark on a person's face, without leaving any evidence of your retouching.

Whilst it would be possible for you to use the paint tools for this type of work, results often tend to look artificial as they lay down flat colours. Fortunately the right textures can be achieved through a cloning process.

The tool which performs this task is the Rubber Stamp.

①   Select the Rubber Stamp tool.

②   Choose Clone (non-aligned) in the Rubber Stamp Tool Options palette.

③   Find an area of the image you wish to sample.

④   Hold down [Alt] and click the centre of the area.

⑤   Click-drag over the defect. A cross hair will appear over the previously sampled area to assist in the retouching process.

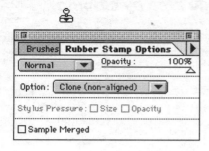

+ The non-aligned clone enables you to work repeatedly with the tool, regardless of how many times you take your finger off the mouse button.

—— Retouching colour logotypes ——

Although logotype designs may differ radically, they usually have several properties in common: designs are hard-edged, colours are flat (matching Pantone or CMYK specifications) and backgrounds are white or transparent.

These properties are often degraded in scans and they need to be re-established by retouching and tonal and colour adjustment.

If transparency is important, this can be achieved in a number of ways, depending on the final medium.

For multimedia images, it's achieved by using ink effect controls within authoring programs, such as within Macromedia Director and Allegiant SuperCard.

For images destined for web pages, it's achieved by using special programs or when saving in special file formats.

For printed images, it's achieved through the use of clipping paths, although redrawing a logotype from scratch using a draw program, such as Adobe Illustrator or Macromedia FreeHand may be a better route to take. See Chapter 11, *Creating cut-outs*.

The colour wheel

The wheel shows graphically the relationship of the red, green and blue colours in the RGB colour model. It's a highly simplified graphic, as it only shows each component colour at full strength, whereas the pixels in an image can be of any strength.

When pairs of colours are mixed in roughly equal proportions they produce the cyan, magenta and yellow colours of the CMYK model. In varying proportions they produce the colours of the spectrum.

A cross-section of the colour wheel can be presented as a seesaw showing how the opposing colours interact with each other.

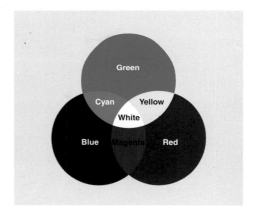

Below: The full spectrum of hues from red, orange, yellow, green, blue, indigo through to violet.
Bottom: The colour seesaw showing opposing colours.

Above: The colour wheel showing the CMYK model interposed over the RGB model (See pages 96–98).

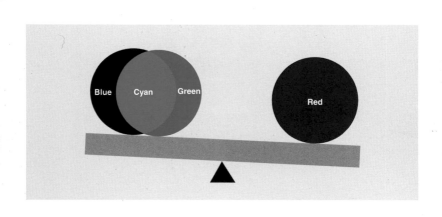

Brightness

Brightness, the degree an image is tonally light or dark, can be adjusted by using the toning tools or by using one of the assisted Adjust controls.

The tools allow you to alter tonal levels locally and are especially useful for increasing detail in critical highlight and shadow areas.

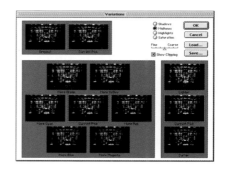

Left: The Toning Tools Options palette. (see page 83). *Bottom:* The image shows extremes of brightness in left and right strips and good brightness in middle strip.

Above: The Variations control gives a preview of brightness options (see page 107).

Saturation

Saturation, the measure of the amount of greyness in a colour, can be adjusted by using the Sponge tool or by using one of the assisted Adjust controls.

The Sponge tool allows you to alter saturation levels locally within images that require high colour fidelity.

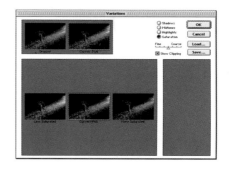

Left: The Toning Tools Options palette (see pages 84–86). *Bottom:* An image with normal saturation in the top strip and low saturation in the bottom strip.

Above: The Variations control gives a preview of how an image will look when saturation is adjusted (see page 111).

Balance

Images which are unbalanced have a preponderance of a hue, such as green.

Balancing an image involves reducing the problem colour or increasing the opposing colours (see the colour wheel and seesaw earlier in this colour section).

Colours can be rebalanced using one of the assisted Adjust controls which allow you to make adjustments at any of three tonal levels.

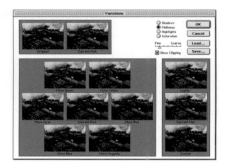

Above: The Variations control gives a preview of how an image will look when individual colours are strengthened (see page 109).

Bottom: An image with unbalanced top and bottom strips and balanced middle strip.

Contrast

Contrast is the relationship between the lightest and darkest areas in an image.

Images which are tonally over-contrasty or flat can be adjusted by using either the Brightness/Contrast or Levels controls.

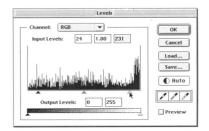

Above: The Levels control enables you to increase contrast with a high degree of control (see page 105).

Bottom: An image with reduced contrast in the left strip, good contrast in the middle strip and increased contrast in the right strip.

Definition

The focus of an image – the degree to which it is sharp or blurred – can be adjusted using the Sharpen and Blur tools or by using one of the sharpening filters.

The tools allow you to alter focus locally and are especially useful for hardening or softening critical edges in subjects.

Left: The Focus Tools Options palette (see page 82). *Bottom:* This image is unsharpened in the left strip, sharpened in the right strip.

Above: The Unsharp Mask filter is a user-definable way of improving edge detail (see page 103).

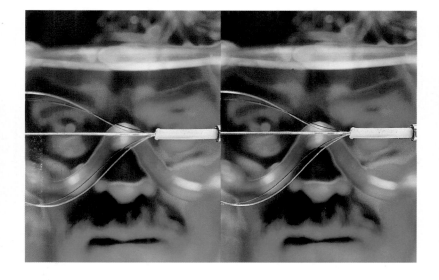

Halftoning images

When a grayscale or colour bitmapped image is printed, its mosaic of pixels is transformed into a screen of halftone dots. The dots are small enough for the eye to merge them together to give a sensation of continuous tones and colours.

The optimum pixel-to-halftone dot ratio is 2:1. This gives four pixels for each monochrome dot and four for each set of process (CMYK) colour dots.

Top: Computer image with close-up of pixels. *Bottom:* Output image with close-up of halftone dots.

Review of
corporate buildings

O
M
to
w
af
h
H
in
fc
as
tr
to
re
er
n
tr

Bit depth and indexing

In bitmapped images, the colour description of each pixel is recorded in one or more bits of information.

The simplest images are 1-bit, giving you black and white $(2^1 = 2)$.

Grayscale images are 8-bit, giving you 256 levels of grey $(2^8 = 2 \times 2 \times 2 \times 2 \times 2 \times 2 \times 2 \times 2 = 256)$.

24-bit colour images give you millions of colours $(2^{24} = 2^8 \times 2^8 \times 2^8 = 16.7+ \text{ million})$.

When 24-bit colour images are displayed on 8-bit systems, either each pixel is assigned its closest match from the standard system palette, or the colour file is indexed.

In the indexing process, the 256 colours most often used in the 24-bit file can be used to make an 8-bit version of the image. This results in an image which looks close to the original, as most colour images include only a fraction of the colours potentially available.

Top: An image with an 8-bit system palette.
Middle: The same image with an 8-bit indexed palette.
Bottom: The image again in 24-bit colour.

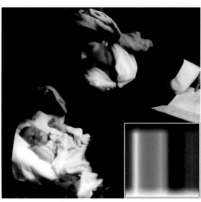

✦   Only line images (Bitmap images in Photoshop) saved in EPS format can have transparent whites without the use of a clipping path.

Retouching steps

The following steps are presented as a general guide to retouching only. Step-by-step instructions on how you use the Adjust controls, filters and tools are covered elsewhere in this book.

Removing halftone screen

Skip this step if a dotted pattern is not present.

●   Apply the Despeckle filter to remove any traces of halftone screen.

Improving tonal values

Complete these two steps for all logotypes with white backgrounds.

①   Make the background white by setting the highlight point within the Levels control.

②   Adjust tonal contrast to match the original using the Levels control.

Removing individual pixels

①   Use the Pencil or Paint brush tool set at a small brush size to paint over individual pixels with the appropriate Current Foreground colour.

②   Use the Eraser tool to erase individual pixels with the appropriate Current Background colour.

Replacing both tones and colours (option 1)

①   Select the Magic Wand tool and set it to a low tolerance value with Anti-Aliased checked.

②   Select individual coloured areas using the tool. The selection border should nearly reach the edges of the existing coloured shape. If it doesn't, reset the tolerance and reselect the area, repeating until until the selection border is correct.

③   Set the Current Background colour to the correct Pantone or CMYK reference.

④   Fill the selection. The fill should spread out to cover the existing colour fully. It will have a slightly vignetted edge.

Retaining tones and replacing colours (option 2)

①   Choose Desaturate in the Adjust sub-menu in the Image menu. This removes all traces of colour but keeps the tones.

②   Select the Magic Wand tool and set it to a low tolerance value with Anti-Aliased unchecked.

③   Select individual tonal areas using the tool. The selection border should reach the edges of the existing tonal shape. If it doesn't, reset the tolerance and reselect the area, repeating until until the selection border is correct.

④   Set the Current Background colour to the correct Pantone or CMYK reference.

⑤   Fill the selection with the mode set to colour. The fill will colour the existing tone.

Reducing the resolution

①   Save the image and make a copy under a different name.

②   Reduce the resolution of the image to the correct final resolution. The drop in resolution will further tidy up edge detail.

—— Undoing retouching work ——

You can correct mistakes in a number of ways in Photoshop.

Undoing a minor action

●   Choose Undo… in the Edit menu.

!   Photoshop can only undo the last action by this means.

Erasing back to saved

You can use the Eraser to paint parts of an image back to a saved file on disk.

①   Select the Eraser tool.

②   Hold down `Alt` (or check Erase to Saved in the Eraser Tool Options palette).

③   Click-drag.

Undoing a series of actions

You can undo a series of actions by reverting to the saved file on disk. It's important to save in a tactical way, anticipating the use of this command, if you use this method.

①   Choose Revert in the File menu. An alert box saying 'Revert to a previously saved version of "…" ?' will be displayed.

②   Click Revert to revert to saved. Click Cancel if you do not wish to revert.

You can use the Rubber Stamp tool to paint parts of an image back to a saved file on disk or back to a stage saved as a Snapshot.

To use the first process, it's important to save in a tactical way as in the case of Revert to Saved.

To use the second process, you need to take a Snapshot in advance at a definite stage in your work.

Painting back to Saved

①   Select the Rubber Stamp tool.

②   Choose From Saved in the Rubber Stamp Tool Options palette.

③   Click-drag over the image.

Painting back to a Snapshot

①   Choose Take Snapshot in the Edit menu. A record will be taken of the whole image.

②   Work on the image.

③   Select the Rubber Stamp tool.

④   Choose From Snapshot in the Rubber Stamp Tool Options palette.

⑤   Click-drag over parts of the image on which you worked.

Summary:

● **Remove dust marks and scratches using the dedicated filter.**

● **Alter the sharpness and brightness of images locally using the focus and toning tools.**

● **Alter saturation locally if colour values are of utmost importance to an image's quality.**

● **Remove unwanted details in photographic subjects using the Rubber Stamp tool instead of the paint tools.**

10

ENHANCING IMAGES

Image deficiencies

Often an image needs tonal, colour and focusing correction to match it to the original subject or to conform to a vision of how the image should look. Correction facilities are built into most desktop scanning programs, enabling adjustments to be made during the scanning process.

However, most people prefer to adjust images after they have been scanned. The separation of the two processes makes better use of your time and enables you to use Photoshop's superior and more interactive assisted controls.

These are some of the properties of originals which determine the quality of scans:

- the colour range of the film stock used to take a photograph

- the lighting of the subject

- the brightness, tonal contrast and saturation of a transparency or print

- the physical size of a photograph or artwork

- the presence of a halftone screen.

The scanning process itself tends to compress the range of tones within images, increasing contrast.

Image sharpening and extreme enlargement when scanning can over-emphasise photographic grain and halftones in subjects, further detracting from image quality.

With all these factors conspiring to degrade image quality, it's not surprising that most images need some tonal and colour correction before they are ready for use.

Image problems

Image problems can be categorised as being tone, colour or noise/sharpness related.

Tone related

Wrong brightness Images appear bleached out (tones too light) or too sooty (tones too dark).

Poor contrast Images appear too flat (tones not differentiated enough) or too contrasty (tones mainly restricted to darks and lights).

Colour related

Unbalanced Images have a preponderance of a hue – too much red or yellow, for instance.

Incorrectly saturated Under saturated images appear weak and washed out – too grey. Highly saturated images appear over rich – 'picture postcardy'.

Focus related

Wrong sharpness Images are grainy and spotty (image too 'noisy') or too blurred (image unsharp).

Fortunately, you can satisfactorily correct most of these deficiencies using Photoshop's Adjust controls and filters.

— Adjustment controls and filters —

Tonal controls

Photoshop's Levels and Brightness/Contrast controls provide you with alternative means of altering the tonal levels within grayscale and colour images.

Adjusting tonal brightness involves strengthening or reducing overall tonal values or mainly midtone values.

Adjusting tonal contrast involves progressively altering tonal values, depending on their degree of lightness or darkness. When increasing contrast, darker tones become darker and lighter tones lighter. The opposite happens when contrast is reduced.

When you operate the assisted controls, both types of adjustment are automatically implemented for you.

Bear in mind the following when adjusting tones.

● Increasing contrast has the effect of reducing the number of greys in an image; thus reducing detail.

● Increasing contrast can give a bit of 'zap' to an image.

● Most images benefit from having a good black and a good white somewhere.

Colour controls and models

Photoshop's Variations, Colour Balance and Hue/Saturation controls all use models to describe colours and to provide a means of altering colour values.

Whilst it's not necessary to be an expert on colour theory to operate these controls, a basic understanding of colour models is desirable if you wish to make proper use of them.

Colour models (or colour spaces, as they are sometimes called) describe the colours we see around us in different ways.

The RGB model

RGB is the model the human eye uses, and not surprisingly, so do scanners, computer monitors and other devices which use light as a colour medium. It's an additive system, with its three colours – red, green and blue – at full strength producing white light, and at minimum strength leaving black.

The CMYK model

The printing industry uses the CMYK model to describe colours created by inks. Unlike the RGB model, it's a subtractive system, with its three colours – cyan, magenta, yellow – at medium strength producing near-black, and all four colours at minimum strength leaving white. Black is included in the model to provide a deep black not attainable by the colours alone because of impurities in inks.

The HSB model

The HSB model is closest to the way we, as humans, perceive colours, as distinct from how our eyes sense colours. It's the easiest model for us to understand and, because of this, it's used to make most colour adjustments.

Unlike the other systems which use hues as a technical basis for colour modelling, HSB describes colours in terms of properties we can easily relate to.

HSB's three component properties are:

Hue colour (red, green, yellow etc).

Saturation intensity or purity of a colour – the extent to which it is not dulled or greyed (ranging from over-rich colour to colourless).

Brightness lightness or darkness of a colour (ranging from very light to very dark).

Balancing colours

Balancing colours is perhaps the hardest type of colour correction to make, as it requires not only good colour perception but also an understanding of the way colours interact with each other.

The colour wheel

This interaction is best explained by referring to a colour wheel showing the relationship of their component colours. See *colour section*.

It's a highly simplified graphic, yet it helps us to understand how colour is balanced within Photoshop. Notice how the spectrum of hues runs around the wheel with roughly equal proportions of red and blue making magenta, roughly equal proportions of blue and green making cyan and roughly equal proportions of green and red making yellow.

Of course, the whole a gamut of hues (all the colours in the rainbow) should really be shown around the wheel, from red, violet, indigo, blue, green, yellow, through to orange and back to red again.

The colour seesaw

Colour balance is best explained by referring to a colour seesaw with red, green and blue weights. See *colour section*.

It was mentioned earlier that when colours are unbalanced, images will have a preponderance of a hue, such as red. To correct the imbalance, you need to alter the strength of the problem colour.

You can do this by reducing the problem colour itself – in this case red – or by strengthening the opposing colour(s), in this case cyan (or both green and blue which make up cyan, if cyan is not represented in a control).

You have this choice because when a colour is strengthened or reduced, the proportion of the opposing colour is altered.

Colour balancing within the controls is automatically restricted to one of three tonal levels: shadows, midtones and highlights. Shadows represent 0–63 on the grayscale, midtones 64–191 and highlights 192–255.

If you wish to balance colours in all three tonal ranges, select each in turn and make the necessary adjustments.

Bear in mind the following when balancing colours.

● Because of the interaction of colours, only fine adjustments are usually necessary.

● Colours can be re-balanced by adjusting the problem colour(s) or adjusting opposing colour(s).

● Colour balancing can affect the saturation of images.

● You can limit colour balance to shadow, midtone or highlight areas.

✦ Black, white and greys are colours as much as crimson and orange. It's just that the component colours which make up the colours are fairly evenly balanced.

Saturation controls

Photoshop's Variations and Hue/Saturation controls provide alternative means of altering saturation. Both of these controls are straightforward to use.

The way Photoshop alters pixel values to adjust saturation, however, is quite complex. When saturation is increased, the strongest component colour(s) increase in value, the weakest component colour(s) reduce in value. Any component colour with a value between the two adjusts itself to maintain a proportional relationship to the other two. The opposite happens when saturation is decreased.

This, of course, is all done automatically for you when you operate the assisted controls.

When adjusting saturation bear the following in mind.

Decreasing saturation can give an image a subtle, colour-wash effect.

Increasing saturation can make an image appear artificial.

Increasing saturation does not necessarily add a lot of extra colour to a fairly monochromatic image.

Enhancing filters

Photoshop's Despeckle and sharpening filters provide the means to remove 'noise' in images and improve image sharpness.

The Despeckle filter removes grain effects, halftone dots and other 'noises' within a scanned image by identifying out-of-character pixels and bringing their values into line with surrounding pixels.

The Sharpen filter focuses blurred images by increasing the contrast of pixels. Sharpen More applies a stronger sharpening effect.

The Unsharp Mask filter gives the illusion of increased sharpness by increasing the contrast of edge detail within images.

When using these filters bear the following in mind.

● High levels of 'noise' within an image can best be avoided if sharpening is disabled during scanning.

A halftone effect within an image can be avoided if a Descreen filter is enabled during scanning.

Removing noise often results in a softer, less focused image.

Oversharpening using the Sharpen or Sharpen More filters can lead to excessive 'noise' in an image.

Unsharp Mask is the best filter for increasing edge detail but it should not be over applied, otherwise its effect can appear artificial.

—— Preparing for correction work ——

Checking pixel values

Display the Info palette at all times when you are doing tonal and colour adjustment work so you can check the colour values of pixels within an image and see the effect of adjustments.

When you make adjustments in any of the Adjust controls, the Info palette displays both before and after values.

①   Choose Show Info in the Window menu.

②   Move the cursor over area of the image you wish to examine. The palette displays the RGB and CMYK (or grayscale) values of the pixels at its location above the image.

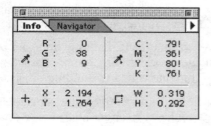

▲   The RGB colour values range from 0 to 255; the CMYK values from 0 to 100%.

Seeing corrections in real time

You can view most tonal/colour corrections made within dialog boxes in real time by enabling Video LUT Animation.

In this mode, colour is not shown quite so accurately on the screen so check Preview in dialog boxes if you wish to view changes more accurately.

①   Choose Display and Cursors… in the Preferences sub-menu in the File menu.

②   Check Video LUT Animation.

③ Click OK.

To use this feature, uncheck Preview in dialog boxes. Press the title
bar of a dialog box with the pointer to view an image in unmodified
form.

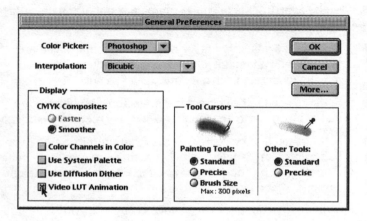

❗ In Photoshop 3.0 choose General... from the Preferences sub-menu in the
File menu to display a similar dialog box.

The correction process

Tonal and colour correction can involve up to seven different
processes, most of them involving a choice of controls.

● Applying the Despeckle filter.

● Applying a sharpening filter.

● Setting highlight/shadow points.

● Adjusting contrast.

● Adjusting brightness.

● Adjusting saturation.

● Balancing colours.

Most images require the resetting of highlight/shadow points.
Other adjustments need only be made if an image has further deficiencies.

When using the controls and filters bear the following in mind.

- Make adjustments in the order as listed and avoid applying the same process more than once. Over-correction leads to inevitable loss of tonal and colour detail.

- Make adjustments to copies of images, not originals, until you have gained confidence in using the controls.

- Don't make adjustments for the sake of it unless you are practising; if an image looks OK, leave it alone, even though it may be incorrect from a technical view point.

- Settings need to be correct in Photoshop's Monitor Setup dialog box prior to any tonal or colour corrections being made.

- Settings need to be correct in the Printing Inks Setup dialog box prior to any adjustments being made to grayscale images intended for printing. See *Preparing images for print* (page 146).

Follow the instructions for each process covered within the following sections until you have gained experience using the controls.

Focusing images

The first item in this section is not strictly a focusing process; it's dedicated to removing unwanted image 'noise'. However, in removing 'noise', it tends to affect image definition.

Removing grain and dots in images

- Choose Despeckle… in the Noise sub-menu in the Filter menu.

Applying Sharpen and Sharpen More filters

Use these filters for improving the focus of blurred subjects or for refocusing images which have become blurred as a result of extreme resampling. Both filters add overall detail to an image by increasing the contrast between adjacent pixels. This can make some images too 'noisy' (spotty).

● Choose Sharpen or Sharpen More in the Sharpen sub-menu
in the Filter menu.

Applying Unsharp Mask filter

Unlike the Sharpen and Sharpen More filters, this adjustable filter
improves edge detail within images, without adding overall 'noise'.
Set the degree of sharpness on images so that they look right on
screen. Use the filter again after setting print levels; in this context
slightly oversharpen images. Oversharpened images will display
'blips' (obvious tonal shifts) at either side of edges. See *Preparing
images for print* (page 146).

① Choose Unsharp Mask... in the Sharpen sub-menu in the
Filter menu. The Unsharp Mask dialog box will be displayed.

② Click on an area of the image in document window. The area
will then automatically show in the dialog box window.

③ Click on + or − to enlarge or reduce the preview image.

④ Set the Radius to .005 of the image resolution (for example,
1.0 for a 200 ppi image), the Threshold to 3 or 4 and the
Amount (degree of sharpness) to an appropriate figure
between 50 and 200%.

⑤ Click OK.

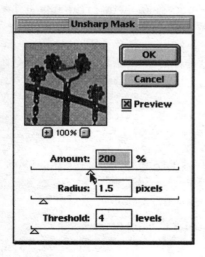

—————— Improving tonal values ——————

Setting highlight/shadow points

Most images should have a full range of tonal values ranging from black in the shadow areas through to white in the highlight areas. In practice, images lose their blacks and whites and these need to be reinstated.

For these images, you can set the points automatically. Photoshop selects the darkest and lightest pixels in an image and adjusts them to black and white. You can also set the points yourself by dragging sliders.

Alternatively, you can set the points using eyedroppers, enabling you to select pixels which you consider to be more representative of the highlight and shadow areas; e.g. you may wish to 'burn out' the whitest areas in an image, such as 'flared' (dazzling) areas on car bodywork and give less-white areas, such as a pale cream shirt, highlight detail.

Some images, of course, won't have a full range of tones; misty subjects are likely to have a predominance of mid tones but no real darks or lights. Skip this process if an image falls into this category.

Either:

① Choose Levels… in the Adjust sub-menu in the Image menu. The Levels dialog box will be displayed.

② Click the Auto button. Both black and white points are set automatically. Alternatively move the left and/or right sliders of the Input levels inward to align with the ends of the histogram.

③ Click OK.

Or:

① Choose Levels… in the Adjust sub-menu in the Image menu. The Levels dialog box will be displayed.

② Select the left eyedropper in the dialog box.

③ Click on the pixel you wish to be the darkest value.

④ Select the right eyedropper in the dialog box.

⑤ Click on the pixel you wish to be the lightest value.

⑥ Click OK.

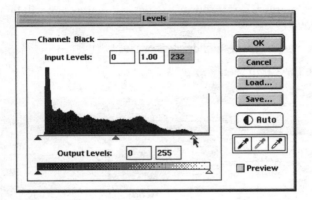

Increasing contrast

Use this control to accurately adjust tonal contrast.

① Choose Levels... in the Adjust sub-menu in the Image menu. The Levels dialog box will be displayed.

② Move the left and/or right sliders of the Input levels inward until the contrast looks right.

③ Click OK.

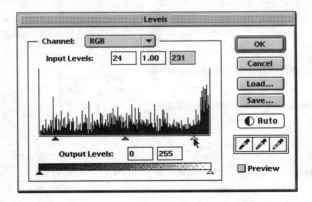

Adjusting brightness and contrast

Use this brightness control to adjust overall brightness levels.

① Choose Brightness/Contrast... in the Adjust sub-menu in the Image menu. The Brightness/Contrast dialog box will be displayed.

② Move the Brightness slider left or right.

③ Move the Contrast slider left or right.

④ Click OK.

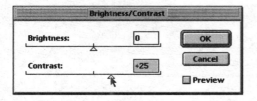

✚ Both brightness and contrast are measured from −100% to 100%.

Adjusting brightness

Use this control to adjust brightness levels within midtone areas.

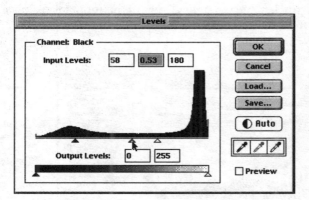

① Choose Levels... in the Adjust sub-menu in the Image menu. The Levels dialog box will be displayed.

② Move the centre slider of the Input levels left or right until the brightness looks right.

③ Click OK.

Adjusting brightness with visual options

Use this alternative control to adjust brightness levels within shadow, midtone and/or highlight areas.

① Choose Variations… in the Adjust sub-menu in the Image menu. The Variations dialog box will be displayed.

② Select Shadows, Midtones or Highlights.

③ Adjust the Fine/Coarse slider to set the degree of difference between the images above and below the Current Pick in the bottom right panel of the dialog box.

④ Click on one of the two images in the bottom right panel to alter the brightness. Each time you click, the Current Pick will be updated in all three panels.

⑤ Hold down [Alt] and click Reset if you wish to undo any changes without closing the dialog box.

⑥ Click OK.

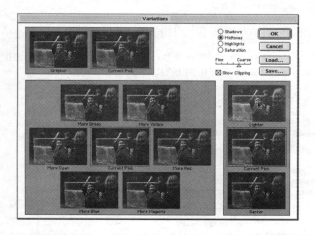

✦ Check Show Clipping to identify images with areas which will be converted to solid black or solid white if chosen (not available when Midtones is selected).

——————— Balancing colours ———————

Whilst colour imbalance is invariably an image-wide problem, it is not always so. Often its effect is more marked in some tonal areas than others. For instance, skin areas may look wrong, whilst at the same time other areas appear perfectly OK. Or everything may look right except for very dark areas of clothing within an image.

Colours may be wrong in localised areas of an image because they are differently lit. Subjects shot partly in tungsten light with daylight film will give images with a strong localised colour cast.

In all these cases, restrict your colour adjustments to the tonal areas which require adjustment, such as shadows or highlights, or alternatively or additionally, mask off areas you don't wish to affect, using the selection tools.

Balancing colours

Use this control to balance colours with your image in full view and scaled at any size.

① Choose Colour Balance... in the Adjust sub-menu in the Image menu. The Colour Balance dialog box will be displayed.

② Click Shadows, Midtones or Highlights.

③ Move the sliders away from a colour name to reduce it and towards a colour to strengthen it.

④ Click OK.

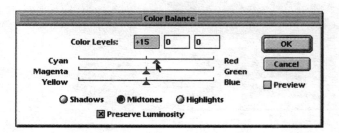

✦ The values at the top of the box show the changing values of the red, green and blue channels respectively.

Balancing colours with visual options

Use this control to balance colours using miniature previews.

① Choose Variations... in the Adjust sub-menu in the Image menu. The Variations dialog box will be displayed.

② Select Shadows, Midtones or Highlights.

③ Adjust the Fine/Coarse slider to set the degree of difference between the images surrounding the Current Pick in the bottom left panel of the dialog box.

④ Click on one of the six images surrounding the Current Pick in the bottom left panel to add more of a colour. Each time you click, the Current Pick will be updated in all three panels.

⑤ Hold down [Alt] and click Reset if you wish to undo any changes without closing the dialog box.

⑥ Click OK.

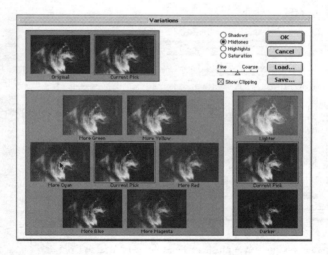

✦ Check Show Clipping to identify images with shadow and highlight areas which will be converted to solid black or solid white if chosen.

Balancing colours with grey subjects

If you know that a neutral grey should be present in an image, such as an area of a grey door, move the cursor over the pixels you judge should be neutral, whatever their brightness.

The Info palette should indicate practically equal values for red, green and blue. If the values are unequal, such as R: 155, G: 175, B: 135, an overall colour cast is present and you may wish to remove it.

①   Choose Levels... in the Adjust sub-menu in the Image menu. The Levels dialog box will be displayed.

②   Select the middle eyedropper.

③   Click on a pixel which you consider should be a neutral value. The pixel values will be equalised to remove any traces of colour. All other midtone pixels within the image will be adjusted on a relative basis.

④   Click OK.

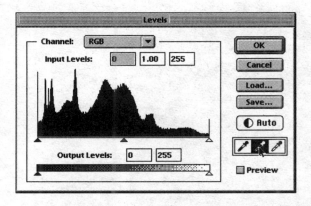

▲   Close in on the greyer pixels in the image by pressing Command-Space.

The eyedropper can be pre-set to colours other than grey by double-clicking on its icon and selecting Custom. The default colour is Pantone Cool Grey 8 CV.

Adjusting saturation

Adjusting saturation using visual options

Use this control to adjust saturation using miniature previews.

①   Choose Variations... in the Adjust sub-menu in the Image menu. The Variations dialog box will be displayed.

②   Select Saturation.

③   Adjust the Fine/Coarse slider to set the degree of difference between the images surrounding the Current Pick in the bottom left panel of the dialog box.

④   Click on one of the images on either side of the Current Pick in the bottom left panel to alter the saturation. Each time you click, the Current Pick will be updated in both panels.

⑤   Hold down [Alt] and click Reset if you wish to undo any changes without closing the dialog box.

⑤   **Click OK.**

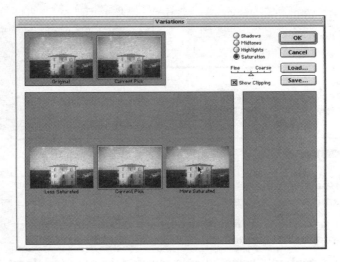

▲   Check Show Clipping to identify images with areas which will be become over-saturated if chosen.

Adjusting saturation

Use this control to adjust saturation with your image in full view and scaled at any size.

① Choose Hue/Saturation… in the Adjust sub-menu in the Image menu. The Hue/Saturation dialog box will be displayed.

② Check Preview.

③ Moving the Saturation slider to the left reduces the saturation, to the right increases saturation.

④ Hold down [Alt] and click Reset if you wish to undo any changes without closing the dialog box.

⑤ Click OK.

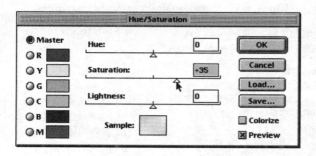

▲ Check Colourize to create a monotone effect or add colour to a grayscale image which has been convered to RGB.

Summary:

● Image problems are tone, colour or noise/sharpness related.

● Up to seven different processes can be involved in image correction.

● Photoshop's assisted colour controls use models to describe and provide a means of altering colour values.

11

CREATING CUT-OUTS

This chapter covers:

●   the Pen tools
●   the Paths palette

You can cut out parts of images in Photoshop so that their backgrounds become completely transparent. This is a useful technique if you wish to overlay images within a DTP or multimedia document as any underlying elements show around their shaped edges.

Cut-outs act as a effective visual foil to squared-up images but they are also a useful way of eliminating unsightly backgrounds.

To create cut-outs for the screen, it's only necessary to give images a white background. You can then use the Ink Effect controls within authoring programs to specify the white areas to be transparent, or the transparency controls within certain web file conversion programs.

If you wish to cut out images on layers within Photoshop, select the areas you wish to be transparent using the Magic Wand tool and delete them.

For printed images, cut-outs are achieved by using clipping paths which effectively mask off areas within an image you wish to be transparent. In this case, there is no need for you to blank out any areas.

Clipping paths are necessary because grayscale and colour images are opaque even in their white areas, unlike line images which can have transparent whites, if saved in EPS format.

+ Paths used as a basis for clipping paths can be converted to normal selection borders. This is useful way of creating a very accurate selection border around part of an image.

Creating clipping paths

Creating a path

Clipping paths are made from specially drawn paths created with the Pen tool.

Image without clipping path.

The same image saved with a clipping path.

①   Choose Show Paths... in the Window menu. The Paths palette will be displayed.

②   Select the Pen tool.

③   Click or click-drag the pen to create a path around part of an image.

④   Finally click on the first anchor point you created. A circular icon will appear as you move the Pen tool towards the point. If this icon does not appear, then you are trying to connect to the wrong point.

!   In Photoshop 3.0 the Pen tool is in the Paths palette.

✚   You can draw a path within a path if you wish to create transparent holes within cut-outs.

Saving a path

①   Choose Save Path in the Paths palette menu. The Save Path dialog box will be displayed.

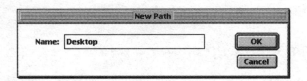

②   Name the path, such as 'Desktop'.

③   Click OK.

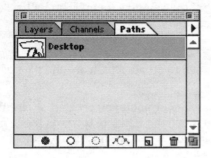

! When a path is saved and on (showing), it is not protected from deletion.

Creating a clipping path

① Create and save a path.

② Choose Clipping path in the Paths palette menu. The Clipping Paths dialog box will be displayed.

③ Select the pen path you have saved in the Path pop-up menu. Enter 5 in Flatness field.

④ Click OK.

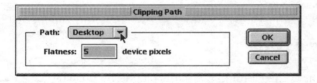

! Save a document with a clipping path in EPS format for QuarkXPress version 3 or later and TIFF format for Adobe PageMaker version 6 or later.

Saving images with clipping paths

Images with clipping paths need to be finally saved in TIFF format for inclusion in PageMaker documents and EPS format for inclusion in QuarkXPress documents. See *Preparing images for print,* page 146.

Using the Pen tool

Creating straight and curved segments

Create a path by clicking or click-dragging with the Pen tool. Clicking the Pen tool creates a straight line segment that ends in a corner anchor point; click-dragging the Pen tool creates a curved segment with an associated smooth anchor point, complete with direction handles.

As you click-drag to create a curved segment, adjust the length and angle of the leading direction handle (the one which the pen tool is controlling) to create a trailing segment of the right curvature.

▲ Check Rubber Band in the Pen Tool Options palette to preview a path as you move from point to point.

The Pen tool works in the same way as its counterparts in Adobe Illustrator and Macromedia FreeHand. If you have not used the pen tool in either of these two programs, you might find the following toy boat analogy useful when drawing curved segments.

Imagine when you draw curves that you are pulling a toy boat along in a pond. As you click-drag, it's as though you are pulling a string attached to the boat. As you 'pull', a curved segment is formed, like the wake of a boat. By altering the length and angle of the 'string', the curve of the 'wake' is altered. When you are happy with the curve, release the 'string'.

When drawing paths bear the following in mind.

● View at a scale that allows you to follow a path accurately.

● Create only as many anchor points as you need to draw a path, especially in the case of smooth points.

● Position smooth anchor points at the tops and bottoms of curves by click-dragging from these positions.

● Always close paths (connect to the first point) as the intention is to 'mask' areas of an image.

● Avoiding creating anchor points over direction handles, as it leads to confusion.

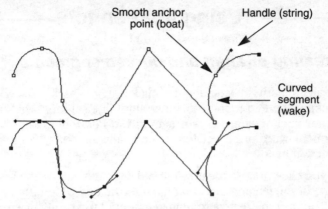

The upper path is in the process of being drawn, from left to right. The lower path shows how the direction lines of curve points are tangential to the curves they describe.

The pen tools: Pen, Add-anchor-point, Delete-anchor-point, Direct-selection. Convert-anchor-point

Altering paths

Moving an anchor point

①   Select the Direct-selection tool or, with any of the other Pen tools active, press 🌐

②   Click-drag point.

Adjusting a curve segment

①   Select the Direct-selection tool or, with any of the other Pen tools active, press 🌐

②   Either: click-drag curve segment.

     Or: click on point and click-drag end of direction line.

Adding/deleting an anchor point

●   Select the Add-anchor-point tool/Delete-anchor-point tool and click where you wish to add/delete an anchor point.

Changing a smooth point into a corner point

● Select the Convert-anchor-point tool and click on a curve point.

Changing a corner point into a smooth point

● Select the Convert-anchor-point tool and click-drag on a corner anchor point to draw out direction lines.

Extending a previously deselected open-ended path

● Select the Direct-selection tool or, with any of the other Pen tools active, press ⌘

● Select the Pen tool and click on end point.

Turning off a previously saved path

● Choose Turn Off Path in the Paths palette menu.

Turning on a previously saved path

● Click on path name in the Paths palette.

! When a path is saved and on (showing) it is not protected from deletion.

Creating a selection border from a path

① Create and save a path.

② Click the Make Selection icon in the Paths palette menu. A selection border will be created.

③ Choose Turn Off Path in the Paths palette menu.

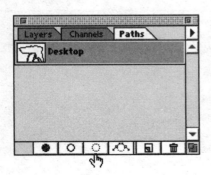

Turning selections into Pen paths

①   Create a selection border using one of the selection tools

②   Click the Make Work Path icon in the Paths palette.

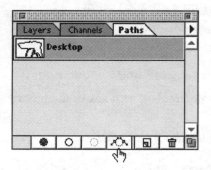

❗   In Photoshop 3.0 the Pen tools are in the Paths palette.

Summary:

●   **Use clipping paths to mask off areas you wish to be transparent.**

●   **Work in a high magnification when drawing with the Pen tool so you can follow the profile of the subject more easily.**

●   **Draw a pen path as a way of making an very accurate selection border.**

12

MONTAGING IMAGES

This chapter covers:

- the Apple Clipboard
- the Select menu
- the Layers menu and palette
- the Layers Mask
- the Transform function
- the Save a Copy dialog box

You can easily combine different images within a single Photoshop document. The images can be copied from other documents or simply moved or copied to new positions within the same document.

If you are creating a complex montage, you can enlarge the area of a document to give yourself more working space. Alternatively you can work from scratch within an empty document.

To assist in the accurate positioning of images, you can add ruler guides to mark out image areas.

Montaging work invariably involves the Apple Clipboard. In both Photoshop 3.0 and Photoshop 4.0, this feature is directly linked to the Layers function but in different ways.

In Photoshop 4.0, pasted images are automatically placed on transparent layers of their own. In Photoshop 3.0, they are automatically floated above underlying imagery.

Either way allows you to alter the attributes of pasted images before merging them with other images or artwork.

Layers are an extremely important Photoshop feature. They enable you to experiment freely with complex montages without you having to create separate versions of documents. They also allow you to test out and apply image graduations easily with their Layer Mask function.

Layered documents can only be saved in the native file formats of Photoshop 3.0 or later, which can't be imported by other programs. When an image is ready for use, you save a flattened copy in a format of your choice or flatten the image you are working in.

! See Chapter 3, *Opening and saving images* for how to create an empty document and Chapter 5, *Viewing and resizing images* for how to create extra working space around an image.

———————— **Pasting images** ————————

Moving and copying images

Moving and copying images is primarily done using the Apple Clipboard (a short-term storage area assigned for this purpose). Any image which you cut or copy is automatically placed on the Clipboard.

However many times you paste, the image will remain on the Clipboard until another image is cut or copied.

Moving an image using the Clipboard

① Select the whole image or the part of the image you wish to move, by using one of the selection methods described in Chapter 7, *Selecting areas and filling*. Choose Cut in the Edit menu.

② If you wish to paste within another document, move to the document. Otherwise skip this step.

③ Choose Paste in the Edit menu. The image will be pasted on a new layer above the previously active layer (or background). If a new layer is already present, empty and active, it will be pasted on this layer.

④ Reposition the image, as necessary, using the Move tool.

✚ A cut selection exposes the current background colour, if any.

Copying an image using the Clipboard

① Select the whole image or the part of the image you wish to copy by using one of the selection methods described in Chapter 7, *Selecting areas and filling*. Choose Copy in the Edit menu.

② If you wish to paste within another document, move to the document. Otherwise skip this step.

③ Choose Paste in the Edit menu. The copy will be pasted on a new layer above the previously active layer (or background). If a new layer is already present, empty and active, it will be pasted on this layer.

④ Reposition the image, as necessary, using the Move tool.

! An image pasted into another document will take on the resolution of the host document, resulting in a change of dimensions of the pasted image if the resolutions differ.

▲ If you have cut or copied a very large area, copy a small area afterwards to reduce the size of the image on the Clipboard.

Altering the attributes of layers

The way pasted images on a layer blend with underlying images can be altered using the Layers palette.

Altering the opacity of a layer (or floating image)

① Choose Show Layers in the Window menu.

② Move the slider on the Layers palette.

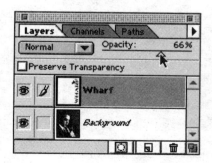

Altering the mode of a layer (or floating image)

①   Choose Show Layers in the Window menu.

②   Choose an option in the Mode pop-up menu.

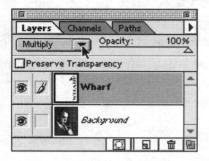

Blending modes

The modes alter the way pixels within a layer or floating selection blend with the underlying image.

Normal/Threshold replaces the pixels of the base colour with the blend colour. This is the usual mode.

Dissolve randomly replaces pixels with the base colour and the blend colour, based on the opacity at any pixel location.

Multiply adds darker tinted values only to the base image, creating a similar effect to overlaying transparencies on a light box.

Screen bleaches colours in the base image. This is the inverse of Multiply.

Overlay multiplies or screens depending on the base colour, but maintains the lightness and darkness of the base image.

Soft Light darkens or lightens base pixels depending on the blend colour. The effect is similar to shining a diffused spotlight on the image.

Hard Light multiplies or screens, depending on the blend colour. The effect is similar to shining a harsh spotlight on the image.

Colour Dodge brightens base pixels to reflect the blend colour.

Colour Burn darkens base pixels to reflect the blend colour.

Darken only changes base pixels lighter than the blend colour.

Lighten only changes base pixels darker than the blend colour.

Difference subtracts the blend colour from the base colour or vice versa depending on which has the greater brightness value.

Exclusion produces a similar but softer effect to Difference.

Hue changes pixels in the base image, but saturation and brightness do not change.

Saturation only changes the saturation of the pixels of the base image.

Colour replaces pixels in the base image, but luminosity (brightness) does not change.

Luminosity only changes the luminosity (brightness) of pixels in the base image. This is the inverse of Colour.

Merging two layers

Use this process to merge a layer with an underlying layer.

①   Click on the layer name or thumbnail in the Layers palette (if not already selected).

②   Choose Merge Down in the Layer menu.

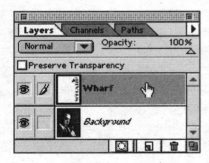

❗   When merged, pasted layers assume the opacity and mode of the layer with which they are merged.

Floating images

Parts of images can be moved or copied without using the Clipboard. Images moved this way become floating selections and do not automatically form a new layer. In Photoshop 3.0, images pasted from the Clipboard also become floating selections.

①   Select the part of the image you wish to move, by using one of the selection methods described in Chapter 7, *Selecting areas and filling*.

②   Click-drag the selection using the Move tool. Hold down $\boxed{\text{Alt}}$ to copy a selection. The image will be floated above the background or layer.

③   Reposition the floating image, as necessary, using the Move tool.

+   A moved selection exposes the current background colour.

Blending floating images

The way a floating selection blends with underlying images can be altered using the Layers palette as described earlier.

Once defloated or deselected, an image's opacity and mode can only be altered as part of a layer.

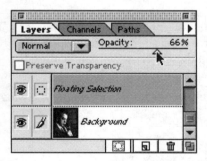

Removing fringe colours around a floating selection

Pasted images sometimes include unwanted colours at their edges. You can replace these fringe pixels by nearby pure colours.

① Choose Defringe… in the Matting sub-menu in the Layer menu. The Defringe dialog box will be displayed.

② Enter a value in the Width field.

③ Click OK.

Deselecting floating selections

Either:

● Choose None in the Select menu.

Or:

● Create a new layer. The selection will be merged with the new layer (in Photoshop 3.0 only).

Defloating selections

● Choose Defloat in the Layer menu.

✦ Deselecting blends and deselects in one operation; defloating blends yet keeps the image selected.

Pasting within selection borders

① Select part of the image into which you wish to paste the current contents of the Clipboard.

② Choose Paste Into in the Edit menu. The image will be pasted within the selection border. An additional icon appears to the right of the thumbnail in the Layers palette indicating the presence of floating image.

③ Reposition the floating image, as necessary, using the Move tool.

Controlling layers

When you are following the steps in this section, merge images onto any layers you create yourself so you can more easily gauge the effect of any operations.

Adding a new blank layer

Either:

- click the New Layer icon at the bottom of the Layers palette.

Or:

- hold down [Alt] and click the New Layer icon at the bottom of the Layers palette. This way you can pre-select options for the new layer.

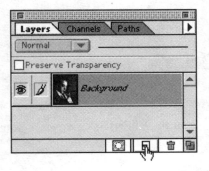

Copying a layer from one document to another

- Click-drag a layer from the Layers palette of the active document to within the document window of the target image.

Selecting a layer

- Click on the layer name or thumbnail in the Layers palette. The paint brush icon denotes the layer is selected.

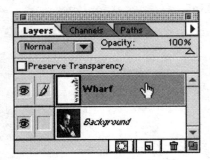

Removing a layer

● Click-drag the layer name or thumbnail into the miniature Wastebasket in the Layers palette.

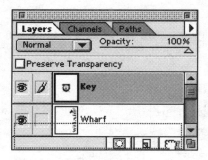

Changing the order of layers

● Click-drag the layer name or thumbnail up or down within the Layers palette.

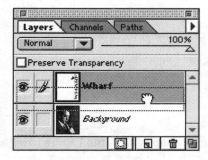

Converting a background into a transparent layer

① Double-click Background in the Layers palette. The New Layer dialog box will be displayed.

② Enter a name in the Name field, a value in the Opacity field and select an option in the Mode pop-up menu. All three can be changed later if you wish.

③ Click OK.

Adding a background to a layer only document

①   Click the New Layer icon in the Layers palette. The New Layer dialog box will be displayed.

②   Choose Background in the Mode pop-up menu.

③   Click OK.

———— Working on layers ————

Painting on fronts and backs of layers

You can limit paint and editing effects to opaque areas on the front of a layer and also paint on the back of a layer.

Keeping transparent areas free from paint effects

①   Select the layer and check Preserve transparency in the Layers palette.

②   Use the paint tools in the normal way, painting across the edge of images to see the masking effect of this feature.

Painting on the back of a layer

①   Uncheck Preserve transparency in the Layers palette.

②   Select a paint tool.

③   Choose Behind in the Mode pop-menu in the Options palette.

④   Use the paints tool in the normal way, painting across images with clear (transparent) areas to see the effect of this mode.

Deleting areas of an image on a layer

① Select the layer.

② Uncheck Preserve Transparency on the Layers palette.

Either:

③ click-drag over the image using the Eraser tool.

Or:

③ make a selection border and press [Delete].

Graduating images within layers

By adding a mask to a layer, you can easily experiment with image graduations, only applying them you if you are happy with the effect.

Adding a layer mask

① Select the layer in the Layer palette to which you wish to add a mask.

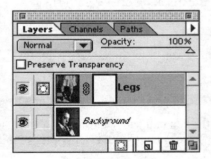

② Choose Reveal All in the Add Layer Mask sub-menu in the Layers palette menu. An additional thumbnail appears to the right of the Layer thumbnail, indicating the presence of the mask.

+ The current foreground and background colours will automatically revert to black and white whilst a mask is selected.

Graduating an image

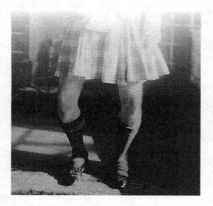

①   Select the Layer Mask, if it is not already selected.

②   Select the Gradient tool.

③   Click-drag over the area of the image to be graduated.

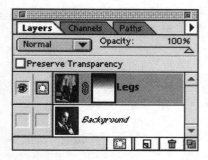

▲   It's best to have underlying layers visible to see the full effect of any masking work.

You can switch between the mask and its accompanying layer at any time, by clicking on either thumbnail in the layers palette.

You can paint and edit parts of an image or the whole of an image while the Mask thumbnail is present.

Applying the graduated mask

① Select the mask.

② Choose Remove Layer Mask... in the Layer menu. The Remove Mask dialog box will be displayed.

③ Click Apply.

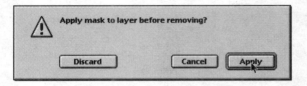

———— **Transforming images** ————

You can scale, rotate, skew, distort, flip or apply perspective to selections using the Transform commands or, in the case of Photoshop 4.0, by also using the Free Transform function.

Whichever method you use, you can preview the effects before applying them.

If you are planning to use more than one transformation effect, such as skew followed by distort, it's best to use the Free Transform method, if it is available.

Free Transform enables you to switch between transformations 'on the fly', i.e. you can preview a series of effects without implementing each in turn. This speeds the transformation process and – more importantly – allows multiple effects to be implemented in one operation.

Resampling usually takes place during a transformation, resulting in pixels being added or deleted. If all the operations are made in one go, resampling take place only once, resulting in the minimum loss of detail.

When transforming selections, it's best where possible to work on layers.

Using the transform commands

① Select the area of the image to be transformed.

② Choose an option in the Transform sub-menu in the Layer menu. Handles will be added to the border.

③ Click-drag a handle to transform the selection (apart from rotation).

④ Move the pointer to the edge of the transform border (but away from one any handle) and click-drag to rotate.

⑤ Select the Move tool to implement the effect.

❗ In Photoshop 3.0 the transformation effects are in the Effects sub-menu in the Image menu.

Using the Free Transform function

① Select the area of the image to be transformed.

② Choose Free Transform in the Layer menu. Handles will be added to the border.

③ Move the pointer to one of the handles of the transform border and hold down [Control]. Choose an option in the pop-up menu.

④ Click-drag a handle to transform the selection (this does not apply for rotation).

⑤   Move the pointer to the edge of the transform border (but away from one any handle) and click-drag to rotate.

⑥   Repeat steps 3 and 4 for each transformation.

⑦   Select the Move tool to implement the effect.

!   In Photoshop 3.0 the transformation effects are in the Effects sub-menu in the Image menu.

▲   Instead of choosing a command from the pop-up menu, hold down the Command key to distort a selection, the Command and Alt keys to skew a selection (using a side handle) and the Command, Alt and Shift keys to create a perspective with the selection.

—— Merging and flattening layers ——

Merging and flattening layers

If you are using a lot of layers within an image, it's a good idea to merge layers when they needn't remain separate and thus reduce the file size of a document and to speed processing times.

When your montaging work is complete, all layers will finally need to be flattened (integrated with the background) to produce a composite image. This is best done to a copy of an image rather than the original, so you can return to an unflattened version of a document at any time should you need to revise it.

There are two main differences between merging layers and flattening an image, as follows.

●   A merged transparent background retains its transparency whilst the background of a flattened image always becomes opaque.

●   Flattened images discard their invisible layers, merged layers have no effect on other layers if made temporarily invisible.

Merging layers

① Click or click-drag 'eye' icons to the left of the thumbnails in the Layer palette to hide those layers you do not wish to merge.

② Choose Merge Visible in the Layers palette menu.

Flattening an image

Either:

① make visible only those layers (including the background) you wish to include in the flattened image.

② Choose Flatten Image in the Layers pop-up menu. An alert box saying 'Discard hidden layers?' will be displayed if any layers are invisible. Click OK.

Or:

① make visible only those layers (including the background) you wish to include in the flattened image.

② Choose Save a Copy… in the File menu in the Layers pop-up menu. The Save a Copy directory dialog box will be displayed.

③ Enter a new document name, overwriting the existing name.

④ Choose an option other than Photoshop 3.0 in the Format pop-up menu. Flatten image will automatically be checked.

⑤ Select a drive and folder in which to save the file.

⑥   Click Save to save the flattened document. Click Cancel if you wish to abort the routine.

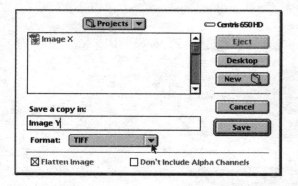

❗   Layers are automatically flattened when converting an image to a different mode, such as from RGB to CMYK.

Summary:

- **Paste multiple images into documents to compose montages.**

- **Create layers within a document to give you the freedom to experiment with compositions and effects.**

- **Adjust the opacity and mode of images by using the Layers palette controls.**

- **Use layer masks to create graduated images.**

- **Scale, flip, skew, rotate and distort images using the transform function.**

- **Create a flattened copy of a layered document if you wish to save in a file format other than Photoshop 4.0 or 3.0.**

13

ADDING TYPE
AND BORDERS

This chapter covers:

- the Type Tool dialog box
- the Border dialog box
- the Stroke dialog box
- the Feather Selection dialog box

Entering type

When you enter type in Photoshop it's immediately bitmapped at the resolution of the image and cannot be edited as type. Because of this, it's best to devote a special layer to type so that any alterations are easier to implement.

Entering type

① Create and name a new layer. See Chapter 12, *Montaging images*.

② Position the layer at the top of the Layer palette.

③ Select a foreground colour.

④ Select the Type tool.

⑤ Click on the image where you wish the type to begin. The Type dialog box will be displayed.

⑥ Enter text in the lower scroll box using the Return key to create new lines.

⑦ Check Show Font and Size to see the text formatted.

⑧ Choose an option in the Font pop-up menu.

⑨ Enter values in Size, Leading and Spacing fields.

⑩ Select attributes, as required, under Style but check Anti-aliased for smooth-edged type.

⑪ Check Anti-aliased for smooth-edged type.

⑫ Click OK. The text will appear as a floating selection border, filled with the current foreground colour.

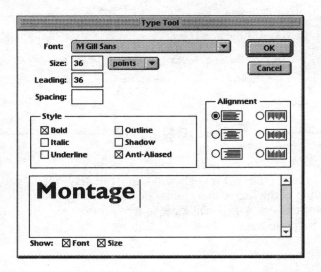

❗ Text in the Type dialog box will automatically wrap at the end of each line but will set as a single line unless the Return key is used.

Selecting and spacing characters

Both the following procedures refer to the floating selection borders created using the Type tool.

Deselecting characters within active text areas

①   Keep the Type tool active.

②   Either: hold down ⌘ and lasso the characters to be deselected.

    Or: hold down `Shift` `⌘` and lasso the characters to remain selected.

Adjusting spacing between selected characters

①   Deselect the character(s) you do not wish to space, using one of the methods described above.

②   Either: hold down `Shift` and click-drag the character(s).

    Or: use the Arrow keys.

—— Creating borders and panels ——

Creating borders

Borders around selections can be created in one of two ways in Photoshop. You can create a vignetted (soft-edged) border using the Border command or a hard or soft-edged edge stroke using the Stroke command.

The edges of a stroke are defined by the Aliasing of the selection around which its formed. A stroke also has positional and blending attributes which a border hasn't.

Selecting a border surrounding a selection

①   Choose Border… in the Modify sub-menu of the Select menu. The Border dialog box will be displayed.

② Enter a value in the Width field.

③ Click OK.

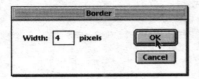

Moving a selection border without moving its contents

● With any of the selection tools active, click-drag the selection border.

! In Photoshop 3.0 hold down the Command and Alt keys.

Creating a stroke around a selection or layer

① Choose Stroke... in the Edit menu. The Stroke dialog box will be displayed.

② Enter a value in the Width field.

③ Click an option under Location.

④ Enter a value in the Opacity field and choose an option in the Mode pop-up menu.

⑤ Click OK.

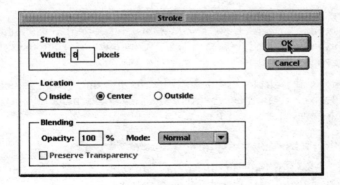

Creating panels

You can place panels behind images to give a sense of depth or to group together different images visually. Panels are easily created using the Marquee tool. The elliptical version offers both soft and hard edges through its Anti-Aliased control.

Whether you are panelling a number of images or just one, it's best to devote a special layer to panels so that any alterations are easier to implement.

Creating panels

① Create and name a new layer. See Chapter 12, *Montaging images.*

② Position the layer beneath the layer containing the image(s) in the Layers palette.

③ Select the Marquee tool you wish to use, setting options in the Marquee Tool Options palette.

④ Select the panel area.

⑤ Fill the selection in the normal way.

Creating offset panels

① Follow steps 1 and 2 under *Creating panels* (previous page).

② Select the Marquee tool you wish to use, setting options in the Marquee Tool Options palette.

③ Select the panel area.

④ With any of the selection tools active, click-drag the selection border to an offset position.

⑤ Fill the selection in the normal way.

! In Photoshop 3.0 hold down the Command and Alt keys when click-dragging the selection border.

Giving vignette edges (soft edges) to panels

① Follow steps 1 to 4 above.

② Choose Feather... in the Select menu. The Feather Selection dialog box will be displayed.

③ Enter an amount in the Feather Radius... pixels field.

④ Click OK.

⑤ Fill the selection in the normal way.

Summary:

● **Enter type using the Type tool on a layer of its own.**

● **Create borders using the Border or Stroke commands.**

● **Create panels using the Marquee tools, giving them vignetted edges using the Feather command.**

14

PREPARING IMAGES FOR PRODUCTION

This chapter covers:

- the TIFF Options dialog box
- the EPS Format dialog box
- the Page Setup dialog box
- the Print dialog box
- the Indexed Colour dialog box
- the GIF 89a Export dialog box
- the JPEG Options dialog box
- the PICT File Options dialog box

Images need to be in the correct mode and their data must be saved in appropriate file formats before they can be inserted into host documents, whatever the medium used.

The mode is determined by the delivery medium and colour availability, i.e. whether images are to be printed or viewed on screen and how many and which colours are to be used.

The choice of file format is limited by what a host document can accept. Depending on their purpose, format types takes into account such factors as colour fidelity, image quality, file size and data transfer/decompression times.

For printed images, bitmap, grayscale, duotone and CMYK are the standard modes with PICT, TIFF and EPS the main format types.

For screen images, RGB is the standard mode with PICT, JPEG and GIF some of the most popular format types.

Three of the file formats mentioned employ compression alogoriths to reduce file sizes on disk and to improve data transfer times: GIF and TIFF use the LZW algorithm (in the case of TIFF it's a user option); JPEG has its own compression system which is lossy, whilst the LZW system is lossless. Data is lost in the former to achieve its higher levels of compression.

It's not possible in this section to cover all production scenarios, as there are so many DTP, presentation and multimedia programs in use today and technical standards are changing all the time.

Therefore the following discussions are limited to selected processes; if your particular need is not covered, you may at least be able to gain an understanding of general principles from those that are included.

!   Avoid compressing TIFFs for production images.

—— Preparing images for print ——

Continuous tone images intended for printing need special tonal adjustments to compensate for the distortion of tonal levels in printed halftones.

Output settings need adjustment to prevent detail being lost in highlight and shadow areas. Input settings need adjustment to compensate for the darkening of midtones.

The effect of the adjustments is to reduce the contrast of images, to lighten shadow areas and to darken highlight areas. Adjusted images may not look good on screen but will reproduce well in print.

Furthermore, RGB images need to be converted to CMYK, the standard process colours used for reproducing colour images. The conversion process takes into account print factors, including the choice of printing ink and the amount of dot gain on press.

All modes need saving in either PICT, TIFF or EPS format.

Use TIFFs wherever possible as they are very reliable and they're also smaller than EPSs.

Use EPS only if you require transparent whites (limited to Bitmap mode only), if an image has been converted to duotone or an image includes a clipping path and it's the only format your program will accept with this feature.

Use PICTs only if files are small, if they are either line or grayscale and if you wish to embed them within host documents. Try to avoid using PICTs for RGB images unless your output is restricted to a QuickDraw printer. CMYK images can't be saved in PICT format.

The saving of images in PICT format is covered under *Preparing images for multimedia projects* later in this chapter (page 159).

✦   QuarkXPress is one program which requires images with clipping paths to be saved in EPS format.

Setting print levels for continuous tone images

①   Choose Levels... in the Adjust sub-menu in the Image menu. The Levels dialog box will be displayed.

②   Enter a value between 1.25 and 1.75 in the central Input Levels field for colour images instead of or to supplement a vlue entered in the Printing Inks Setup dialog box. See *Saving RGB images in TIFF format* (page 148).

③   Enter the following values in the Output Levels fields.

    Newsprint: 30 and 225; uncoated stock 25 and 230; coated stock 12 and 243.

④   Click OK.

▲   Apply Unsharp Mask if an image loses definition as a result of this adjustment.

Saving bitmap or grayscale images in TIFF format

Saving a file as a TIFF

① Save the image, choosing the TIFF format. The TIFF Options dialog box will be displayed.

② Click Macintosh and uncheck LZW Compression.

③ Click OK.

Saving RGB images in TIFF format

Specifying the Printing Inks Setup and altering the mode

① Choose Printing Inks Setup... in the Colour Settings sub-menu in the File menu. The Printing Inks Setup dialog box will be displayed.

② Choose SWOP Coated, Uncoated or Newsprint in the Ink colours pop-up menu, depending on the paper the document will be finally printed on and enter a vlaue recommended by your printing company in the Dot Gain... % field.

③ Click OK.

④ Choose CMYK in the Mode sub-menu in the Image menu.

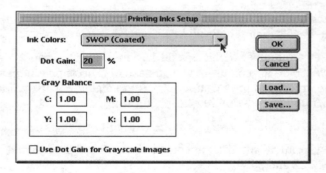

! Ensure the correct dot gain amount is entered and check Use Dot Gain for Grayscale Images when making tonal corrections to grayscale images intended for printing. Otherwise leave unchecked.

Saving the file as a TIFF under another name

① Make a copy of the image by using the Save As procedure. Add the letters cmyk after the name (this is optional) and choose the TIFF format.

The TIFF Options dialog box will be displayed.

② Click Macintosh and uncheck LZW Compression.

③ Click OK.

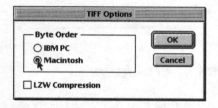

❗ Macromedia FreeHand is not able to import clipping paths with images. To create a clipping path, you must place the TIFF in the Freehand document and paste it inside a suitably-shaped closed path created with the Pen tool.

▲ Place the original RGB file in a safe place in case you wish to return to it later.

Saving bitmap or grayscale images in EPS format

Saving a file as a EPS

① Save the image choosing the EPS format. The EPS Format dialog box will be displayed.

② Choose Macintosh (8-bits/pixels) in the Preview pop-up menu.

③ Choose a path in the Path pop-up menu, if you wish a clipping path to be included.

④ Uncheck Include Halftone Screens and Transfer Functions.

⑤ Click OK.

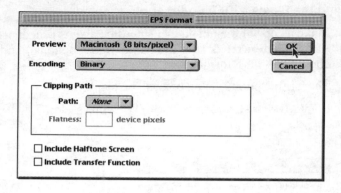

Saving RGB images in EPS format

Specifying the Printing Ink Setup and altering the mode

● Specify the Printing Inks Setup and alter the mode, as for RGB TIFFs.

Saving the file as an EPS under another name

① Make a copy of the image by using the Save As procedure. Add the letters cmyk after the name (this is optional) and choose the EPS format.

The EPS Format dialog box will be displayed.

② Choose Macintosh (8-bits/pixels) in the Preview pop-up menu.

③ Choose Off (single file) in the DCS pop-up menu and ASCII or Binary in the Encoding pop-up menu.

④ Choose a path in the Path pop-up menu, if you wish a clipping path to be included.

⑤ Uncheck Include Halftone Screens and Transfer Functions.

⑥ Click OK.

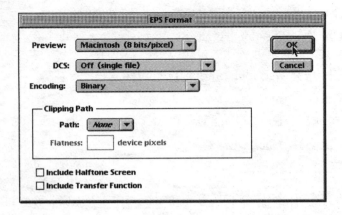

!   Choose ASCII for images to imported into Macromedia FreeHand.

▲   Place the original RGB file in a safe place in case you wish to return to it later.

✦   EPSs support transparent whites in bitmap mode only.

Preparing images for composite printing

RGB images need to be converted to CMYK for direct composite printing from Photoshop and files, whether grayscale or CMYK, ideally saved in TIFF format.

Ensure the correct ink colour is chosen in the Printing Inks Setup dialog box before altering the colour mode of a document. See *Specifying the Printing Inks Setup and altering the mode* (page 148).

Proofing images from Photoshop

The following covers some of the controls used for proofing documents with pictures on a black and white or colour laser printer.

Checking the Page Setup

①   Choose Page Setup... in the File menu. The Page Set-up dialog box will be displayed.

②   Choose the paper size to be printed on.

③ Select the image orientation to suit the document.

④ Check Calibration bars, if a progressive grayscale bar (or progressive colour bar in the case of CMYK) is required.

⑤ Check Registration Marks, if required.

⑥ Check Corner Crop Marks, if required.

⑦ Click Screen.... Check Use Printer's Default Screens.

⑧ Click OK. Click OK.

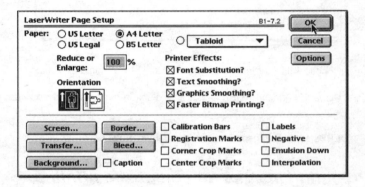

Printing the image

① Choose Print... in the File menu. The printer's dialog box will be displayed.

② Enter the number of copies required within Copies.

③ Under Encoding, check Binary.

④ Click Print.

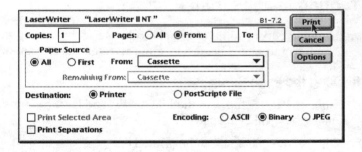

—— Preparing images for screen ——

Colour images for screen display should remain in RGB mode but their bit-depth can be reduced from 24 to 16 or indexed to 8 or less.

16-bit colour images display 65 536 colours, giving you museum quality – 'photo-realism' – so there's invariably no need to maintain images in 24-bit.

Indexed images can display up to 256 colours. Because their colour range can be drawn from any one of the 16.7 million plus colours available, this can compensate for their restricted palette.

Indexing not only gets the best colour out of 8-bit display systems; by converting files to 8-bit or less, it reduces file sizes, thereby increasing display speeds.

Grayscale and bitmap images can remain in their modes although the former can be indexed, if converted first to RGB mode.

All images for screen display need to be set at a resolution of 72 ppi (dpi).

Whether indexed or not, images need to be saved in appropriate file formats.

Images for web pages are usually saved in GIF, JPEG or Progressive JPEG format, all of which are hardware-independent. A further format called PNG is intended to replace or supplement GIF in the near future, and offers better colour support amongst a wealth of other features.

Images for multimedia projects developed on the Macintosh are usually saved in PICT format.

✦ Indexing is a system which refers files to a colour table for their colour range. The number of colours a file refers to depends on its bit-depth The colour table can include any of the 16.7 million or so colours capable of being displayed on 8-bit monitors, not just your Macintosh's 256 system colours.

Preparing images for web pages

When saving or exporting images for web pages, it's important to choose the format with the most appropriate compression system.

GIF's LZW system works best on graphic images containing horizontal runs of flat colour, such as icons and logotypes. It works less well with images containing lots of pixel variation, such as photographs. JPEG's system, on the other hand, is good at dealing with pixel variation but is poor at handling flat areas.

As regards decompression times, GIF images generally take a shorter time to decompress than JPEG images.

Both GIF and Progressive JPEG offer interlacing, the former also offers transparency.

GIF versus JPEG/ProJPEG: overview

	GIF	JPEG	ProJPEG
Compressing flat colours	good	poor	poor
Compressing photographs	poor	good	good
Decompression speed	fast	slow	slow
Ability to interlace	yes	no	yes
Ability to have transparency	yes	no	yes
Support for 24-bit colour	no	yes	yes

Exporting images to GIF format

GIF images are indexed and can be exported from pre-indexed or RGB images within Photoshop.

The former method allows you to manually select the colours you wish to become transparent. The latter method allows you to use the layer and feather commands within Photoshop to define transparency. It also allows you to preview an image at various colour depths (bit-depths) and access special proprietory colour palettes, such as Netscape's 216 palette (cube).

Both methods gives you the option of interlacing.

Whichever method you use, aim to achieve the right balance between colour quality and small file sizes.

The best colour rendition is achieved by using the Adaptive palette (which weights the colours in the palette based on how frequently they are used in the original image). However, images on the same web page may have their colours remapped on monitors with only 8-bit colour support.

Both Adobe's Web 216 CLUT palette and Netscape's 216 palette are restricted to 216 colours but their limited colour range has the advantage being consistent in all situations.

▲   One way to avoid the remapping of images using the Adaptive palette is to reduce the overall number of colours in a group of images to 256, e.g. each one of a group of three images could be 6-bit, giving 64 colours each.

Creating a GIF from an indexed image

① Open an RGB image.

② Choose Indexed… in the Mode sub-menu in the Image menu. The Indexed Colour dialog box will be displayed.

③ Either: choose Adaptive in the Palette pop-up menu. Choose an option in the Colour Depth pop-up menu if you wish to further reduce the file size. A reduction in colours is less likely to suit photographic images. If the colour-depth is already less than 8 bits/pixel, choose Exact instead of Adaptive.

Or: choose Web in the Palette pop-up menu.

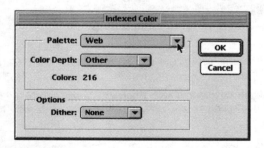

④ Experiment with either None or Diffusion in the Dither pop-up menu.

⑤ Click OK.

⑥   Choose GIF89a Export… in the Export sub-menu in the File menu. The GIF89a Export dialog box will be displayed.

⑦   Check Interlaced, if interlacing is required.

⑧   Select the Eyedropper tool and click on pixels you wish to be transparent. Hold down ⌘ and click to deselect colours.

⑨   Click OK.

⑩   Name the file with .gif extension, locate and open folder in which to save the GIF.

⑪   Click Save.

⑫   Close the original image.

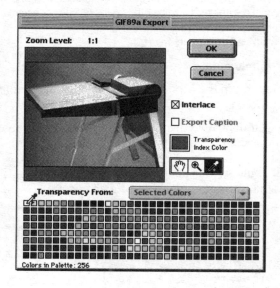

!   In Photoshop 3.0 choose Indexed Colour… in the Mode menu to display this dialog box.

The GIF89a plug-in only works with Photoshop version 3.05 or later. Interlacing and transparency attributes in GIFs only work with some browsers.

▲   To create small files with images using the Web palette, convert the images back to RGB after indexing (completing step 5 in the above process) and create GIFs using the Adaptive palette as described under *Creating a GIF* *from an RGB image*. This way you can further reduce the number of colours in an image and preview its effect in the GIF89a Export dialog box.

✦ The Web 216 CLUT palette (called Web in the Palette pop-up menu) and the latest GIF89a Export plug-in are available from Adobe.

Creating a GIF from an RGB image

① Open an RGB image.

② If you wish to make the image's background transparent, place it on a layer, make the area you wish to be transparent clear and hide the background.

③ Choose GIF89a Export... in the Export sub-menu in the File menu. The GIF89a Export dialog box will be displayed.

④ Either: select Adaptive in the Palette pop-up menu. Choose an option in the Colours pop-up menu if you wish to further reduce the file size (avoid 255 colours). A reduction in colours is less likely to suit photographic images.

Or: click Load. A directory dialog box will be displayed. Use the directory dialog box controls to locate a proprietory palette, such as Netscape's 216 palette. Click Open. The palette will appear in the Palette pop-up menu.

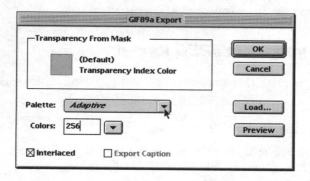

⑤ Click Preview to assess the colour range, Click OK (revise the number of colours and preview again, if necessary).

⑥ Click OK. The Save dialog box will be displayed.

⑩ Name the file with .gif extension, locate and open folder in which to save the GIF.

⑪ Click Save.

⑫ Close the original image.

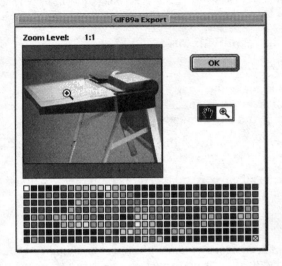

❗ Interlacing and transparency attributes in GIFs only work with some browsers.

✚ The Netscape 216 palette is available from Netscape.

Saving images in JPEG format

JPEG images are either grayscale or 24-bit and can be highly compressed.

Saving the file as a JPEG

① Open a grayscale or RGB image and save in JPEG format. The JPEG Options dialog box will be displayed.

② Under Image Options, choose Low, Medium, High or Maximum in the Quality pop-up menu. These settings alter the degree of data compression.

③ Under Format Options, click Baseline Optimized for better colour quality or Progressive Optimized to give an interlace effect. If you select the latter, choose Fair, Good, Very good or Excellent in the Scans pop-up menu.

④ Click OK.

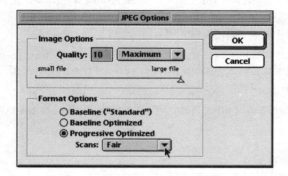

Preparing images for multimedia projects

Although a variety of file formats can be accepted by multimedia programs, in practice the PICT format is most widely used. Macromedia Director, Allegiant Supercard, QuarkImmedia, VideoFusion and Adobe Premiere all support this format.

Images can be 1-bit, 2-bit, 4-bit, 8-bit, 16-bit or 32-bit, depending on the authoring or editing program, image subject and colour strategy you adopt.

If you are partly targeting older computers with only 8-bit colour support, images may need to be indexed to 8-bit or less.

Some programs help to further reduce file sizes by automatically compressing imported images. Others enable you to reduce their bit-depth once imported.

Indexing an image

① Open an RGB image.

② Choose Indexed... in the Mode sub-menu in the Image menu. The Indexed Colour dialog box will be displayed.

③ Choose Adaptive in the Palette pop-up menu if you wish to maintain the best colour fidelity in an image

Or: choose Exact in the Palette pop-up menu if you wish to use the actual colours in the image. This option is only available for images with 256 colours or less.

Or: choose System (Macintosh) or System (Windows) in the Palette pop-up menu if you wish to use the standard Macintosh or Windows colours.

④ Choose an option other than 8 bits/pixel in the Colour Depth pop-up menu if you wish to further reduce the number of colours in an image. Otherwise leave at 8 bits/pixels.

⑤ Experiment with either None or Diffusion in the Dither pop-up menu.

⑥ Click OK.

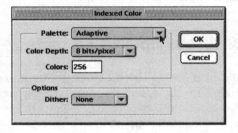

❗ In Photoshop 3.0 choose Indexed Colour... in the Mode menu to display this dialog box.

Saving the file as a PICT

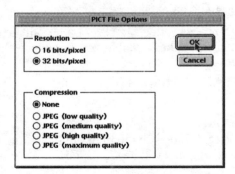

① Save the image choosing the PICT format. The PICT File Options dialog box will be displayed.

②   Click a Resolution and Compression option, as required.

③   Click OK.

Working with indexed images

Since only one set of 256 colours is available on 8-bit monitors at any one time, indexing needs to be planned with care if unpleasant colour shifts are to be avoided.

The complication of displaying images together or in sequence with different custom palettes may outweigh the advantage gained in colour fidelity.

The problem can be removed completely by restricting yourself to the system palette or imposing a single common custom palette throughout a project, covering both content and interface elements.

Alternatively any number of common palettes can be used within a project, as appropriate.

A common palette can be developed and applied within Photoshop, within an authoring program such as Macromedia Director or using the graphics translator DeBabelizer, made by Equilibrium.

Creating a common palette within Photoshop

①   Create a large new blank document.

②   Paste the images into the blank document.

③   Index the combined image using the Adaptive palette with any dither option selected. Click OK.

④   Choose Colour Table… in the Mode sub-menu in the Image menu. The Colour Table dialog box will be displayed.

⑤   Click Save to save the colour table.

⑥   Close the combined image.

⑦   Open one of the original images.

⑧   Choose Indexed Colour… in the Mode sub-menu in the Image menu. The Indexed Colour dialog box will be displayed.

⑨　Click Custom… with no dither. Click OK. The Custom dialog box will be displayed.

⑩　Click Load. A directory dialog box will be displayed.

⑪　Use the directory dialog box controls to locate the saved colour table.

⑫　Click Open. Click OK to apply the palette. The image will be indexed using the colour table.

⑬　Repeat steps 6 to 11 for the other images.

—— Preparing images for slides ——

Images can be output as colour slides using a slide film recorder, which is a device comprising a black-and-white cathode-ray tube attached to a 35 mm or large-format camera.

Most recorders support QuickDraw, the same system which draws the Macintosh screen, so you should have no technical problems arising from this method of output.

Images for slides need to be adjusted to cater for the difference in gamma between monitors and photographic film.

If you are planning to produce a lot of slides from images, it will be worth your while calibrating your system for film output. You can do this by outputting an image to slide without making any special adjustments and then using the Gamma CDEV utility supplied with Photoshop to match the screen to the illuminated slide.

Otherwise, if you are just producing one or two slides, you can use the standard gamma adjustment covered in the following steps.

The effect of the adjustment is to lighten midtone areas severely, making images look far too light when they are viewed on an uncalibrated screen.

All images for slides need to be in 24-bit, RGB mode. A variety of file formats can be used, including Photoshop 3.0, PICT and TIFF (either compressed or uncompressed).

Film recorders measure resolution in terms of image size, such as 4K (4096×2732 pixels). Think of a recorder as having a number of grids, one for each outputting resolution (2K, 4K, 8K etc). To get the best output from a recorder, the image must be equal to or slightly smaller than the dimensions of a grid (in pixels). Otherwise the image will have to be resized. A resolution of 4K, incidently, exceeds the resolution of Ektachrome so a higher resolution adds to processing time without increasing image sharpness.

The optimum image size for 5×4 in transparencies is 4096×2732 pixels, giving an approximate file size of 35 MB and a resolution of 4K. Any ppi resolution will do, as the slide production house will change it to suit their requirements.

The optimum image size for 35 mm transparencies is 2048×1366 pixels giving an approximate file size of 10 MB and a resolution of 2K. As for 5×4 in transparencies, any ppi resolution will do.

Setting gamma levels for slides

① Choose Levels... in the Adjust sub-menu in the Image menu. The Levels dialog box will be displayed.

② Enter 2.2 in the central Input Levels field.

③ Click OK.

Summary:

- **Images need to be in the correct mode and file format for a given use.**

- **Printed images are usually saved in TIFF, EPS and PICT format.**

- **Screen images are usually saved in GIF, JPEG and PICT format.**

- **Images for print and slide production need their output and/or gamma settings adjusted.**

I would like to thank Paul Greenstein for his advice on preparing images for use in web pages and multimedia projects.

15

ALLOCATING MEMORY

This chapter covers:

- the Memory control panel
- the Get Info dialog box
- the Scratch Disk Preferences dialog box
- the About this Macintosh panel

Photoshop is memory-hungry: it needs adequate memory to process large files and to perform complex tasks with sufficient speed and efficiency. This memory can be solely RAM, your Macintosh's built-in memory, or RAM in combination with free space on a scratch disk (a designated hard disk).

Its scratch disk system is always on and normally works best when your Macintosh's own virtual memory system is switched off.

Provided that you have sufficient free scratch disk space, you can allocate to Photoshop an amount of memory that is slightly less than the largest unused block in RAM (taking into account the preferred size of your scanning program and any other programs you wish to run at the same time as Photoshop).

If you do not have much spare disk capacity, allocate to Photoshop an amount that is slightly less than the largest unused block in RAM (taking into account the preferred size of your scanning program).

So if you wish to get the best performance out of Photoshop you will need to address three memory aspects.

- The Macintosh's virtual memory
- Photoshop's scratch disk system
- Photoshop's memory allocation

The Macintosh's virtual memory

Photoshop's scratch disk system works best if the Macintosh's own virtual memory system is switched off.

Switching on the virtual memory

① Choose Control Panels in the Apple menu. Double-click on the Memory icon. The Memory control panel will be displayed.

② Click On under Virtual memory.

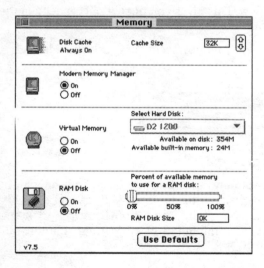

③ Click the On radio button under Modern Memory Manager or 32-bit addressing.

④ Reduce the amount in the Cache Size field to the minimum (this is optional).

⑤ Close the control panel.

⑥ Restart your computer.

Ascertaining free disk space

Ascertaining overall disk capacity

You need to know the capacity of your hard disk, and/or other disk(s) to be specified as scratch disks before you can calculate the amount of free disk space.

① Double-click the disk icon (chosen as a scratch disk) on the Desktop.

② Add up the two figures (in MB) immediately below the title bar of the window. This gives you the overall capacity of the disk.

③ Repeat steps 1 and 2 for any secondary disk and add both totals together.

Ascertaining free disk space

You now need to check how much free space you have on your hard disk, and/or other disk(s) to be specified as scratch disks. Photoshop 4.0 requires a minimum of 20 MB of free disk space, Photoshop 3.0 requires a minimum of 20 MB and Photoshop LE needs a minimum of 10 MB.

① Select the disk icon on the Desktop.

② Choose Get Info in the File menu.

③ Take the figure (in brackets) after Size away from the overall disk capacity figure. This gives you the total amount of space available for scratch disk use.

④ Close the dialog box.

⑤ Repeat steps 1 to 4 for any secondary disk and add both totals together.

Photoshop's memory allocation

You can now allocate the amount of memory you wish Photoshop to use. Photoshop 4.0 requires a minimum of 16 MB of application RAM (32 MB recommended), Photoshop 3.0 a minimum of 12 MB (24 MB recommended) and Photoshop LE a minimum of 8 MB (16 MB recommended).

Altering the memory allocation

① Choose Quit in the File menu, if Photoshop is loaded.

② Choose Finder in the Applications menu on the far right of the menu bar.

③ Locate the Photoshop program icon. If it is greyed return to step 1.

④ Select (click once) the Photoshop program icon.

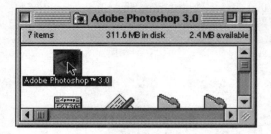

⑤ Choose Get Info... in the File menu.

⑥ Enter an amount in the Preferred size field.

⑦ Close the dialog box.

⑧ Re-load Photoshop in the usual way. The system software will set aside the memory you allocated.

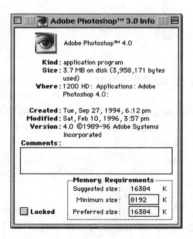

❗ The amount you enter in the Preferred size field must be smaller than the amount of free disk space on your chosen scratch disk(s). See *Ascertaining free disk space*, page 166.

Calculate the preferred size as follows: take the Available built-in memory figure (from the About this Macintosh dialog box or the Memory control panel), e.g. 25 000K, subtract the System Software figure (from the About this Macintosh dialog box), e.g. 5000K, and the Preferred size of your scanner program (from its Info box), e.g. 5 000K. Multiply the figure left by 90%. (25 000 − 5 000 − 5 000 = 15 000. 15 000 × 90% = 13 500)

Photoshop's scratch disks

Photoshop's scratch disk system is always on and is used whenever it's unable to hold a complete image on the computer's RAM.

It 'shunts' data it can't hold on RAM onto disks which you specify for this purpose and these can include your start-up disk (which normally is your internal hard disk) or any external drives, even ejectables. Remember any disk drives you specify need to have sufficient contiguous spare space to act as an efficient medium for this work.

Choosing a scratch disk

① Choose Scratch disks... in the Preferences sub-menu in the File menu.

② Choose an option in the Primary and Secondary pop-up menus.

③ Click OK.

④ Choose Quit in the File menu and then reload Photoshop in the usual way.

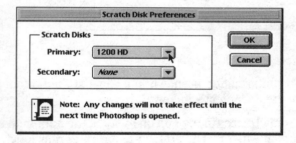

!   Ensure that you have at least as much scratch disk space as RAM allocated to Photoshop. Otherwise you may get a Scratch Disk Full message.

Monitoring memory and scratch disk usage

Monitoring memory usage

You can monitor memory usage when Photoshop is running.

① Choose Finder in the Applications menu on the far right of the menu bar.

② Choose About this Macintosh... in the Apple menu. The About this Macintosh dialog box will be displayed.

The Total (Built In) Memory is measured in K and beneath are listed all the loaded programs and their current memory allocations.

③ Close the dialog box.

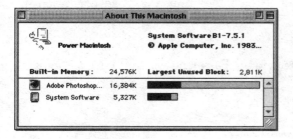

Monitoring scratch disk usage

The scratch size information is shown in a panel at the bottom left hand corner of the document window.

● Choose Scratch Sizes in the pop-up menu at the bottom left of the document window. The first figure indicates how much space Photoshop is currently using. The second figure indicates the total amount of RAM available. If the first figure exceeds the second figure, Photoshop is using the scratch disk(s).

APPENDIX I

—— Photoshop 4.0 and LE ——

Additional features in Photoshop 4.0

Adobe Photoshop 4.0 has additional features to Photoshop 3.0.

Since this book is intended for newcomers to the program, it only includes those features of version 4.0 which make the program either easier to learn or easier to use at a beginner's level.

Therefore you will be able to carry out practically all of the processes covered using Photoshop 3.0.

Photoshop 4.0 includes these additional features:

The Actions palette; Adjustment layers; the Free Transform function; the Navigator palette; guides and grids; custom, multicolour gradients; 48 new effects filters; digital watermarking; web integration.

✚ Adobe can supply an upgrade from Photoshop 3.0 to Photoshop 4.0 for those wishing to benefit from its extra features.

Limited features in Photoshop LE

Many scanners are bundled with Adobe Photoshop LE. This limited edition program lacks some of the features of its fully-fledged counterpart. As a result, you will not be able to carry out some of the processes covered, if you are using this version.

The LE version currently lacks:

Layers; separation output capability and CMYK colour; the Gamut Warning command; the CMYK Preview command; the Alert triangle for Out of Gamut colours in various palettes/dialogs; QuickEdit; the Load/Save Selections commands; paths; the File Info; the ability to open and place Adobe Illustrator files; export formats: paths to Illustrator, QuickEdit Save; all calibration facilities.

✦ Adobe can supply an upgrade from Photoshop LE to Photoshop 4.0 for those wishing to exploit Photoshop's full range of features.

APPENDIX II

Keyboard shortcuts

Tool or key	Plus	Result
Painting		
Eyedropper	`Alt`	Selects background colour
`Delete`	`Alt`	Fills with foreground colour
Any paint/edit tool	`⌘`	Move tool
Misc paint tools[1]	`Alt`	Eyedropper tool
Any paint/edit tool	Number key	Sets paint opacity
Any paint/edit tool	`Shift`	Constrains stroke
Any paint/edit tool	`Caps Lock`	Cross-hair pointer
Eraser tool	`Alt`	Magic eraser, paints with last saved version
Any tool	`⌘`	Removes colour from Swatches palette
Any tool	`Alt` `Shift`	Adds colour to Swatches palette
Any tool	`Shift`	Replaces colour in Swatches palette

1 Airbrush/Pencil/brush/paint bucket/line/gradient tools.

Selecting

Tool or key	*Plus*	*Result*
Marquee	Shift	Constrains to circle or square
Marquee tre	Alt [1]	Draws marquee from cen-
Marq/lasso/wand	Shift	Adds to selection
Marq/lasso/wand	Alt	Subtracts from selection
Marq/lasso/wand	Alt Shift	Connects parts of separate selections
Alt	Click-drag	Moves a copy of selection
← → ↓ ↑		Moves selection in increments of 1 image pixel

Viewing

Tool or key	*Plus*	*Result*
Grabber	Double-click tool	Fits image to full size window
Zoom tool	Double-click tool	100% magnification
Zoom	Click-drag	Magnifies selected area
⌘	−. or +_=	Zooms and resizes window
⌘ Space	Click	Magnifies image when dialog box is open
Alt Space	Click	Reduces image when dialog box is open
Pointer	Click title bar	Shows colours before adjustment in dialog box

1 The Command key in Photoshop 3.0.

Pen tool shortcuts

Tool or key	Plus	Result
Any pen tool	⌘	Move tool[1]
Any pen tool	P	Rotates through pen tools

Other shortcuts

Tool or key	Plus	Result
Any paint/edit tool	⌘ + F	Applies last filter
Any paint/edit tool	⌘ Alt + F	Opens last filter dialog box
Any paint/edit tool	Control + >	Cancels operation
Any paint/edit tool	Space	Grabber tool

Cropping images in Photoshop 3.0

Tool or key	Plus	Result
Alt	Click-drag corner	Rotates crop
⌘	Click-drag corner	Moves crop

1 The pointer in Photoshop 3.0.

APPENDIX III

—————— Glossary ——————

Alert box dialog box on a screen alerting you to all the consequences of a decision you are about to take

Anti Alias addition of pixels with intermediate values at the boundaries of edges to reduce the 'staircasing' effect of a bitmapped representation

ASCII American Standard Code for Information Interchange. Standard format for representing digital information in 8-bit chunks

Binary the base-2 numbering system that most computers use

Bitmap image made up of pixels (or dots)

Brightness amount of white or black in a colour

Bromide photographic paper used by imagesetters for artwork quality prints

Bit smallest possible unit of information. Short for binary digit

Bit depth a measure of the amount of information recorded or displayed for each pixel

Bureau company specialising in printing and/or imagesetting DTP documents: in this book, bureau refers also to a repro department at a printing works and a colour copy shop

Cast overall colour bias

CCD Charge-Coupled Device: a light-sensitive chip-mounted device used in scanners to convert light into an electrical charge

Character generic name for a letter, number or symbol.

Check box small box that works as a toggle for selecting an option. When you click on an empty box, an X appears, turning it on; when you click again, the X disappears and the option is turned off

Chooser desk accessory used to log into devices, such as printers and other computers linked to a network. Also used to enable and disable AppleTalk, Apple's native networking protocol

Clipboard area of a Macintosh's memory that holds what you last cut or copied. Paste inserts a copy of the current contents of the Clipboard

Clipping path a vectored path which masks areas of an image when printed

CLUT Colour Look-Up Table: a colour indexing system used by computers to reference colours if their systems don't support the correct bit-depth to represent all colours

CMYK stands for cyan, magenta, yellow and key (black): the colour model used in the graphic and printing fields

Contone Continuous tone: a photographic print, negative or transparency containing continuous tones

Contrast the relationship between the lightest and darkest areas in an image

Cut-out non- rectangular image

Cursor the pointer or insertion point

Document size in Photoshop, the overall amount of data in an image

Dialog box box on a screen requesting information, or a decision, from you

dpi Dots Per Inch: measurement of the density of information in an image. Also the measurement of the resolution of printers and imagesetters. See ppi

dtp Desktop Publishing

Drive floppy, removable or hard disk

Field in Photoshop, an area in a dialog box or palette in which you enter values

Film photographic film used by imagesetters for colour separations

Floating selection a pasted selection which hasn't yet been blended with the underlying pixels

Folder sub-division (sub-directory) of a disk

Font typeface comprising a collection of letters, numbers, punctuation marks and symbols with an identifiable and consistent appearance

Format way of saving files and transferring data

Gamma measure of how compressed or expanded dark or light tones become in an image

Gamut range of colours available in a particular colour system space (or mode)

GIF Graphic Interchange Format: most widely-supported file format for web pages

Hand tool which allows you to move around a document without using the scroll bars

Grayscale depiction of grey tones between black and white: usually composed of 256 greys

Halftone pattern (or screen) of dots of different sizes used to simulate a continuous tone photograph, either in colour or monochrome. Measured in lines per inch (lpi)

Hue the colour component of colour, such as red or green

I Beam cursor's shape when dealing with text

Image graphic, photograph or illustration

Imagesetter digital phototypesetting machine capable of producing graphic images as well as type on bromide or film. Most imagesetters are PostScript-compatible

Indexed colour a colour system which uses information from a file or from software as a pointer to a table of colours rather than specifying a colour directly

Insertion point blinking vertical line indicating where the next keystroke will add or delete text

Interpolation estimation of values between two known values. Assignment of an intermediate colour to pixel based on the colour of the surrounding pixels

JPEG Joint Photographic Experts Group: pronounced 'Jaypeg'. A set of standards developed for compressing and decompressing digitised images

Keystrokes use of modifier keys with other keys to execute a command

Keypad the numeric keys on the right of the keyboard (extended version)

Leading repeat distance between lines of text, usually measured between baselines

lpi Lines Per Inch: the measurement of a halftone screen

LZW Lempel, Ziv and Welsh: a lossless compression algorithm

Menu list of commands

Modifier keys keys which modify the effect of a character key when pressed. The standard modifier keys are ⌘, Alt, Shift, Control and Caps Lock.

Monochrome tonal original, in shades of only one colour, such as black

Montage collage of images

Original artwork or photographs used as a subject for scanning

Palette small movable box containing commands

Pantone Matching System PMS for short: proprietory colour matching system used in the graphics and printing industries.

Photo litho Photo lithography: the primary printing technology used in the printing industry

PICT Apple's native file format

Pixel Picture Element: the smallest distinct unit of a bitmapped image

Plug-in program which extends the functionality of Photoshop

PNG Portable Network Graphics: colour file format for web pages using lossless compression algorithms

Point unit of measure used in type measurement: there are approximately 72 points to the inch.

ppi Pixels per Inch: measurement of the density of information in an image. See dpi

Process colours the CMYK colours used to reproduce colour photographs and illustrations

Program sequence of instructions that tells a computer what to do: also called software

Printer digital desktop or commercial device for printing or proofing documents primarily using laser, ink jet, die sublimation or thermal wax technologies

PostScript Adobe's page description language used by QuarkXPress and other DTP programs

QuickDraw programming routines that enable the Macintosh to display graphic elements on screen and to output text and images to certain QuickDraw printers.

Radio buttons group of small buttons for selecting a option, only one of which can be on at one time

RAM memory a computer uses to store information it's processing at any given moment

Registration marks marks included on film separations for purposes of colour registration

Remapping rearranging the pixels within a bitmapped image

Resampling adding, deleting or re-arranging pixels within a bitmapped image

Resolution in this book, the amount of data in a scanned image, measured in pixels (or dots) per linear inch

Retouch removal of minor defects within an image

RGB The colour model used by monitors and within multimedia projects, based on red, green and blue

Saturation a measure of the amount of grey in a colour. The higher the grey content, the lower the saturation

Scan bitmapped image created by a scanner

Scratch disk designated disk used by Photoshop temporarily to off-load data it can't hold on RAM

Scroll bars bars equipped with a scroll box and scroll arrows which enable you to scroll vertically or horizontally within windows

TIFF Tagged Image File Format, the defacto file format for saving scanned images

Trim marks lines printed outside the edge of a document page for aligning guillotines

TWAIN generic driver used to access scanning controls from within Photoshop

Window enclosed area on the screen in which a document appears

Vectored drawing or object defined mathematically: sometimes called object orientated

Virtual memory a means of using storage memory on a disk to supplement RAM

Vignette soft edge given to images

Plug-in third part program which extends the functionality of Photoshop

Keys

| Alt | Alt key: modifier key used in conjunction with other keys, often providing an alternative function

| Delete | Back space/Delete key: used to delete selections and, within the Type dialog box, to delete text to the left of the insertion point

| Caps Lock | Caps Lock key: used to turn tool icons into a cross hair

| ⌘ | Command key (with an Apple on it): modifier key used with other keys to issue commands

| Control | Control key: modifier key used in connection with other keys

| Enter ↵ | Enter key: used to close dialog boxes

| Return | Return key: used to separate paragraphs within the Type dialog box and close dialog boxes

| Shift | Shift key: modifier key used to capitalise letters and constrain pointer movement, amongst other things

| Tab | Tab key: used to hide and show palettes

INDEX

Apple, 50, 69, 121, 123, 165, 170, 177, 179, 181
current colours
  altering, 47
  saving, 53
  swapping, 52
  reverting to default, 52
colour models
  CMYK, 3, 49, 51, 84–5, 88–90, 96, 100, 138, 146–52, 172, 177, 180
  HSB, 96–7
  Pantone, 47, 51–2, 54, 88–90, 110, 179
  RGB, 47–9, 84–5, 96, 100, 138, 146–51, 153–54, 156, 158–59, 163, 180
colours
  sampling, 47–48
  mixing, 47–49
  saving, 53
colouring
  gradients, 47, 171
  fills, 173
  text, 3, 140–41, 178–81
correcting
  colour balance, 3, 96–8, 102, 108
  brightness, 3, 8, 24, 93–5, 97, 101, 106–7, 110, 126, 176
  gamma, 106, 147, 162–63, 178
  highlights, 98, 107–9
  midtones, 98, 107–9, 146
  saturation, 3, 8, 84, 92–4, 96–9, 101–2, 111–12, 126, 181
  shadows, 98, 107–9
  sharpness, 3, 77, 94–5, 99, 103, 112
  tones, 72, 89, 94–5, 104, 177

Clipboard., 19–20, 60, 121, 123–24, 127–28, 177
characters
  font, 140, 178
  respacing, 140
  size, 140
  typestyle, 140
cut-outs
  creating clipping paths, 114
  saving clipping paths, 116, 147
borders
  panels, 141, 143–44
dialog boxes
  About This Macintosh, 164, 168, 170
  Border, 141, 144
  Brightness/Contrast, 106
  Colour Balance, 93, 108
  Custom Colours, 52
  EPS Format, 151
  Fill, 64
  General Preferences, 42, 50
  Get Info, 166, 168
  Gif89a Export, 155–56
  Hue/Saturation, 112
  Indexed Colour, 155, 160
  JPEG Options, 158
  Levels, 71, 74, 78, 93, 104–6, 110, 147, 163
  New Document, 14
  Page Setup, 145
  Pict File Options, 160
  Print, 145
  Save Path, 115
  Stroke, 142
  Tiff Options, 148–49
  Type Tool, 139
  Unsharp Mask, 103